meditations
by the sea

meditations by the sea

MARION RAWSON VUILLEUMIER

AN AUTHORS GUILD BACKINPRINT.COM EDITION

Meditations by the Sea

AN AUTHORS GUILD BACKINPRINT.COM EDITION

Published by iUniverse.com, Inc.

For information address:
iUniverse.com, Inc.
620 North 48th Street, Suite 201
Lincoln, NE 68504-3467
www.iuniverse.com

Originally published by Abingdon

ISBN: 0-595-00368-0

Dedicated To:

THOSE KINDRED SOULS IN SMALL PRAYER GROUPS
WHO HAVE HELPED MY PERSONAL PILGRIMAGE IN THE:

LACONIA CONGREGATIONAL CHURCH
Laconia, New Hampshire

THE FIRST CONGREGATIONAL CHURCH
West Springfield, Massachusetts

CRAIGVILLE CONFERENCE CENTER
Craigville, Massachusetts

SOUTH CONGREGATIONAL CHURCH
Centerville, Massachusetts

MAYFLOWER PLACE CHAPEL
West Yarmouth, Massachusetts

Also to the worshippers at
FRIENDS MEETINGHOUSE
South Yarmouth, Massachusetts

Introduction

The salty tang of the sea as I near it never fails to excite me. Some primeval response deep within me seems to well up into my consciousness bringing a joyous anticipation and a quickening excitement. As the ocean itself comes into view with its beckoning, limitless horizon, I have a feeling I have come home.

For the first decades of my life I lived inland with only an occasional glimpse of the sea. Those are shining moments in my memory. Those first waves can still be felt splashing over my feet, then receding, taking the sand from under my teetering soles. I remember too the delight of finding a myriad of differing shells and taking them home wrapped in a damp, disintegrating brown paper bag. Treasures on my pink, painted bureau, they kept alive my seaside memories between visits.

When married life began and longer vacations were part of a parsonage family's schedule, our path inevitably led to the sea. Though we would travel the nation's highways and by-ways from its rolling plains to its mountain passes, we would always spend the last week or so by the sea. We need the sea, we told ourselves, to refresh our bodies and infill our souls before plunging back into parish life. Somehow the God who created and programmed this mysterious, watery mass seemed closer when we rested at its shore. Like sponges we soaked up reminders of his presence for the winter to come.

What joy it was to learn one day that we were to live by the sea. That vast, eternal body of water that encompasses the globe would always be in our view. We would see it in the gray morning when the line between sea and sky is indiscernible. We would see it in the sparkling noonday sun. We could gaze at its moonlit path when night had come. We would be constantly reminded by this ocean that we could see, of the ocean of blessings we could not see but know to be always available; for the God who made it is far greater and his resources even more unlimited.

One day we followed a ponderous furniture truck over the Sagamore Bridge high above the Cape Cod Canal to a low Cape Cod–style house. A twelve-foot glass wall in the living room framed a tiny creek winding its way to Nantucket Sound in the distance.

As we settled into this atmosphere of salt, sea, and pines I felt as if we had found a haven—like a ship after a long voyage sailing thankfully into home port.

In the two decades since, I have found spiritual riches immeasurable by its shores. With heartfelt thanks to all who have nourished my Christian life and to my clergyman husband, Pierre, I share these riches now with you.

I must also express my appreciation to all who aided in the research for this book and especially to Marian Logan who typed the manuscript.

1980

Addendum

After living for twenty-nine years in view of the sea, I now live without the view, though I am thankful the sea is still only about a mile away. I am close enough to hear the mournful sound of the Nantucket ferry as it docks in nearby Hyannis.

In these intervening years many changes have occurred. My husband Pierre and daughter Virginia have preceeded me into the life everlasting. But I still have the comfort of sons Pierre and Louis as well as many other relatives and friends. Also, through these years the sea I can view and the everlasting sea of God's love that undergirds us all, have been unfailing supports.

Thus I welcome being able to share again the spiritual riches I have found at the ocean's shore.

Marion Rawson Vuilleumier
West Yarmouth, Massachusetts
February 2000

CONTENTS

The Vast, Eternal Sea

*Can you find out the deep things of
    God?
Can you find out the limit of the
    Almighty? . . .
Its measure is longer than the earth,
and broader than the sea.*
                    —Job 11:7, 9

Many people are at first awed by the vastness of the ocean's stretch into infinity. They stand gazing toward the horizon, unable to comprehend that here there is no end. It is hard to understand that this ever-moving mass continues in a soft curve around the globe, unceasingly flowing into itself.

In her recent book *House by the Sea*, poet and novelist May Sarton was struck by this thought. She commented that she lives "under the powerful spell of the sea" but that it was different than she had imagined. She had thought she would be influenced by the rising and falling tides. Instead she was gripped by the "wide spaces" and the "shining, still, blue expanse."

One's first thoughts of God are like that. How can he be here, there, everywhere? How can he be on call to all of his children at one and the same time? How can he respond to a prayer from a Chinese man while listening to an Eskimo's plea? What if there are voices calling to him from beyond this small planet as the universe flows on into infinity?

It is comforting to gaze at one of God's creations that is literally global yet very real right here, right now. We can splash in its waves and feel its coolness on our body, as people in other lands are doing so simultaneously. While we are perfecting our breaststroke on a summer's day surfers in Hawaii are riding the crests of the waves.

The vast, eternal sea can sometimes be frightening. I recall

13

carrying a very small gray cat to the shore for her first close look at the ocean. After one horrified glance at more water than she had ever imagined, the cat leaped out of my arms wild-eyed and fled for the safety of the car. We laughed uproariously; yet later, soberly I reflected that often our first thoughts of God can be as terrifying when we really open our mind to his awesome power, his infinite capabilities, and the concept of eternity.

Fortunately, familiarity with one of God's creations, the sea, can teach us something of the nature of God, help us grow in faith, and alleviate our fears.

O God, our Creator and our Father, thank you for the ocean—its length, its breadth, and its depth. Thank you also for its qualities which remind us so much of you. As the ocean's invigorating waters strengthen us physically, may the ocean of your love with its boundless spiritual resources give us the inner strength needed to meet life's demands; in the name of Christ. Amen.

A Mesmerizing Experience

If I take the wings of the morning, and
dwell in the uttermost parts of the sea;
even there shall thy hand lead me, and
thy right hand shall hold me.
—Psalm 139:9-10 KJV

After the first sense of awe passes, one is caught by the sense of constancy and peace exuded by the sea. To be sure, there is activity and tumult. The waves crash forward and then recede.

The tide ebbs and flows. There is constant motion, though it may not be readily apparent on the calmest of days.

Watching this ceaseless activity, this constant motion, is a mesmerizing experience. Gradually one relaxes, lulled by the monotony of the repeated sounds and identical acts. Cares fall away. The calm present seems more vivid than the pulsing round of daily activities, than the turbulence of the worrying problems.

Daphne duMaurier felt this, for she wrote in her autobiography, *Myself When Young—The Shaping of a Writer,*

> Utter peace comes upon me when out to sea. No cares, no feelings, no restlessness, no repressions; just calm, with scarcely a thought. . . . I sat for a long time at the open hatch by the slip watching the harbour. I felt absolutely pure, like a soul at rest. It seemed to me that everything I looked upon was beautiful and eternal, and that no trace of anything was ever lost.

The reality and availability of God comes more into focus during these moments. We always know intellectually that he is there, ready to hear our every cry, always listening to our prayers. Yet sometimes in our busyness we let a forest of things to do and a bramble of cares screen out our sense of his Presence. By the sea we regain our perspective, we push our way through the seemingly impenetrable forest of worries and come closer to God. We feel his nearness, and we drink in his peace.

The Scriptures take this experience one step further. God is not limited to this stretch of seashore. His right hand will hold us, says the psalmist, in the uttermost parts of the sea.

Charles Lindbergh, the first man to fly alone across the Atlantic and a man with a long, distinguished career in aviation, had this certainty. At his request Psalm 139:9-10 was cut into the cement covering his grave, which is by the seashore on the island of Maui in Hawaii.

It is a certainty we too can know as we refresh ourselves by the sea. It is a helpful remembrance long after we have left the ocean's edge. Just a whiff of salty tang as we pack away the bathing bags or a handful of sand falling out of the beach pails will remind us when the sea is far away that it is a symbol of relaxation and of the availability of our God. A snatch of the mesmerizing experience returns, and we are calm again.

Our loving Father, whose care for your children extends to the uttermost parts of the sea, grant us the peace and serenity that comes from loving you better. Help us to rest so in you that our spiritual roots may delve deeper and deeper into thy resources. Help us to be faithful in our devotions so this closeness we attain by the seaside will be ready to sustain us when we again face the turbulence of daily life; in Jesus' name. Amen.

An Artist Never Satisfied

I want you to know, brethren, that our fathers were all under the cloud, and all passed through the sea, and all were baptized into Moses in the cloud and in the sea.
—I Corinthians 10:1-2

The sea is an artist that is never satisfied. It is constantly at work adding and subtracting to the shoreline as if it is trying to create a perfect, finished drawing. It adds a stretch here, cuts a cove there, and sometimes amidst a freezing storm cuts away whole sections of land. One wonders what the ultimate shore will be like, what is the goal the sea is working to accomplish. Could it be similar to the way God works to perfect his human children?

The poet William Lindsay thought so when he wrote "The Waves' Confessional."

> The billows up the broad bay crawl and creep,
>   With white locks o'er bowed shoulders streaming far
> And faltering, confess in whispers deep
>   Their sins of passion and their deeds of war;
> While hermit pines, in somber mantles clad,
>   Bend from the cliffs with ceaseless sob and sigh,
> And shrive the penitents, with arms outspread,
>   Ere on the saffron shore they fall and die.

The apostle Paul saw our lives in much the same manner when he noted that our spiritual fathers passed under the dark cloud and through the threatening sea with Moses on their way to the Promised Land. To reach their goal they went through much travail. In a sense we are like that constantly eroding shore and like our Old Testament forefathers. We are passing through a school of life, a cleansing period. We can hope we are changing and improving as we travel toward our Promised Land.

It is not easy. We are human. We are in an imperfect world that is full of temptations. There are things we should do that we have not done. Have we visited that sick neighbor in the rest home who longs for a friendly call? Have we baked a cake for that family whose young mother is ill? Have we telephoned our friend to compliment her on an especially fine job as chairman of the choir robe committee?

There are also things we should not do that we have done. Why did we stay glued to that time-wasting movie on television rather than write the long-delayed letter? Why did we let that morsel of gossip slip between our lips when it would have been kinder to let it remain unsaid?

The ways of the sea remind us that God always gives us another chance. We can confess, repent, and begin again. Like the sea, we should never be satisfied but continually endeavour to improve under the gentle guidance of the Holy Spirit.

Our Father God, who is eternally loving and forgiving, help us to continually strive to be more Christ-like. When we fall and fail, help us to acknowledge this, confess our faults, and begin again; in the name of our Lord Jesus. Amen.

A Not-So-Silent World

*Yonder is the sea, great and wide,
which teems with things innumerable,
living things both small and great.*
—Psalm 104:25

"For ages people have believed the ocean depths to be silent," writes Francine Jacobs in her recent book *Sounds in the Sea.* "This vast ocean space that covers almost three-fourths of our planet was called 'The Silent World!' But now scientists are learning that the depths are not still. There are sounds in the sea."

People who listen with hydrophones can hear the patter of raindrops on the surface of the water or the groaning of shifting ice floes. During storms, waves crash noisily, and ocean currents collide. Earthquakes split and crack the earth's crust in deep ocean trenches producing an incredible, crunching din.

By far the most interesting sounds come from the creatures that live therein. Young whales yelp, bark, whistle, and trill. Tiny shrimps snap and crackle. Spiny lobsters, or crawfish, produce squeaky noises by rubbing their antennae together, thus frightening their enemies. Male ghost crabs hiss, while male fiddler crabs thump. The continuous sound of barnacles' feeding can sometimes be heard miles away under the sea.

Our own silence is something like that of the sea. A beginner in meditation is somewhat frightened of silence. We are used to a noisy world. Radios are turned on as soon as we awaken. The television blares whether we watch it or not. One of a variety of electric helpers seems always to be humming. If it isn't the furnace, it's the refrigerator or the air conditioner. Outside is just as bad. In some cities the noise pollution is so high it is continually being measured. A prolonged silence in this culture is sometimes scary.

Yet a serious searcher will find, after the first practices have begun, that the silence comes alive. Time speeds by. There is an infilling that satisfies an inner yearning. It is even a richer period if others are sitting in silence with you. Quakers have always known this and sometimes travel miles to worship in silence with like-minded folk.

The ocean depths, ageless and mysterious, are teaching us that knowledge and understanding are rooted in silence, whether in the ocean or in our soul. Sir Walter Scott said, "Silence is deep as is eternity, speech is shallow as time." By sinking into silence, we are put in touch with spiritual forces of inestimable help, and we find in the innermost parts of the soul a not-so-silent world.

Heavenly Father, who art rooted and grounded in silence, help us to hear your voice in our silence. Help us to set aside time for listening to you. Fill us with thy spirit and thy power that we may in turn be powerhouses to others. May we thus be worthy to be called disciples of our Lord Jesus, who left his busy world to seek the renewing silence of solitude when living here on earth; in his name. Amen.

Exhilaration and Rejoicing

> Let the heavens rejoice, and let the
> earth be glad; let the sea roar, and the
> fulness thereof.
> —Psalm 96:11 KJV

There is an ocean's roar that is exhilarating. It comes after a storm when the surf is high. Wave after wave crashes onto the beach as if glad to be reprieved from the storm and happy to be performing its appointed task.

The poet William Chase Greege captured this well.

> The breakers pound upon the yellow strand
> The stony shore is moist with dashing spray
> The frothy waves make sport like lambs at play,
> And turbid billows roll with seething sand.
> I hear the ocean's roar on every hand,
> And watch the ceaseless sweep along the bay;
> I see the dark green watery masses sway,
> And surge, and unrelenting, rush to land.

When we plunge into these high-spirited waves we are exhilarated. There is that very first gasp when the cold water splashes against our warm limbs. Then comes excruciating excitement that increases as bit by bit our body sinks into the ocean. Finally, gratefully, our whole self is submerged.

Exhilaration continues as we bob up and down, tossed by the incoming waves. We count them, watching for the seventh, which for some reason is presumed to be the highest. Occasionally a mild undertow trips us and we tumble under the waves, emerging spluttering but triumphant, having beaten Neptune's children on their own surf.

Our lives are like that ocean. The days and years that lie ahead are unfathomable. There is no charted path. The waves, the tides, the undertow of life, push and pull at us in ways we cannot predict. Sometimes we are tossed about until we are breathless.

We can look ahead into the unknown and worry, concerned because we cannot see the pathway. But worrying creates a state of emergency, according to Dr. Jack Downing, in a recent interview in *Prevention Magazine*. The word *worry* means "to tear apart." When we worry we tear ourselves apart. How much better to accept life as we do the unpredictable, exhilarating ocean. We can sway with the currents, rejoice in the excitement, and rise laughing after a spill. The ocean can teach us many things, and not the least is the way to face life.

Gracious God, lord of the vast ocean of our future, help us to put our trust in thee each day and face life rejoicing. Help us also to be thankful that when life buffets us, your undergirding arms are always present to faithfully carry us forward; in Jesus' name. Amen.

Ebb and Flow

He divideth the sea with his power.
—Job 26:12 KJV

I used to fret because my energy seemed so unpredictable. One day I would awaken with the dawn, planning what I would write, whom I would telephone, where I would go. Each hour, items on the list were crossed off. Satisfaction mounted with completed tasks. As I sank into slumber that night I murmured thankfully, "It has been a good day."

Another day I would awaken lethargically, groping my way into the morning slowly. Finally, after morning coffee, I would face the day's chores determinedly but unenthusiastically. Every task seemed an effort. Where was the energy of those good days?

Then we vacationed by the seashore. Our travel trailer rested on a bluff overlooking Nantucket Sound just above a wide beach. Night and day we heard the inexorable ebb and flow of the waves. In sun and shower, evening or morning, high tide or low, the waves energetically pushed shoreward then peacefully fell back into the deep. Ever forward. Ever backward. Ever forceful. Ever restful. There was a continuous ebb and flow.

Gradually the conviction grew as the days passed by that our lives are like those waves, and we should follow their example. When energy rises powerfully within us we should ride its crest, accomplishing all we can until the energy is spent. Then, when it is dormant we should relax, rest, and await its onset. There must be no fretting, because this is an eternal pattern.

Job, who suffered much and still kept his faith in God, may have had this in mind when he said, "He divideth the sea with his power." The obvious meaning, of course, is the awesome power of God, mighty enough to split the sea in two. But I like

23

to think that Job had a second lesson in mind. God divides his sea constantly into an ebb and flow revealing that energy that has spent itself must retire and recoup. After it rushes it must relax.

Thornton Burgess, best known for his animal stories, also wrote poetry. He grew up near the sea and observed its secrets. In his poem "Beside the Sea" he wrote:

> Prithee tell me if you may
> What it is the breakers say
> As they pound upon the shore
> With a deep and hollow roar.

Though Burgess never finds the secret in this poem, I think I know now what the breakers say. They are calling humans to follow the waves' age-old example. Rush and produce, then rest and regenerate. Ebb and flow.

Our Father God, thank you for the example of the waves. When our energy does not flow, help us to rest and wait, confident that it will rise again. Help us also to dedicate all our energies to working within thy will; in Jesus' name. Amen.

All Things Touch All Others

*And when they heard it, they lifted
their voices together to God and said,
"Sovereign Lord, who didst make the
heaven and the earth and the sea and
everything in them."*
—Acts 4:24

Throughout the pages of the world's literature, from the writings of Greek philosophers to the present day, there runs a golden strand of thought that observes that all humans and all of nature are but parts of one whole, and whatever touches one section affects all.

Nowhere is this better dramatized than in the sea. A bottle thrown into the Atlantic Ocean, directed by the currents, and pushed by the waves may find itself in the Pacific. An undersea quake in one part of the sea produces tidal waves in another part of the globe. Pollutants washed down rivers near industrial centers are found in fish caught near the Arctic Circle. All life is indeed interconnected.

In a perceptive book for youngsters called *The Mermaid's Three Wisdoms*, Jane Yolen touches on this same theme. She weaves a magical story about Melusina, a mermaid who has no tongue, and Jasmine, a land girl who is deaf. One of the three wisdoms of the ancient merfolk helps them to understand one another. It is, "Know that all things touch all others, as all life touches the sea."

As we reflect on this by the seaside it is easy to understand the part played by the sea in touching all life. This body of water covers three-fourths of the world's surface and is literally everywhere. It is much harder to understand that our actions affect all others.

Perhaps we do make an impression on those with whom we come into direct contact, one admits.

If we are dour and unhappy, we send out negative vibrations to others. If we do this continually, we soon find folks avoiding our company. Sometimes it is done unconsciously as when our friends make other plans not realizing they feel uncomfortable in our presence. Other times it is a recognized act. "She makes me feel downhearted," they comment. "Let's not invite her."

Fortunately this works in reverse. A genuinely cheerful individual seems automatically to leave smiles and good humor in his or her wake. A positive personality who says thanks for a job well done or gives a compliment about someone's pleasing appearance sends out "good vibes," and the ripple effect of the good humor engendered is amazing.

One sensitive observer likened humanity to a spider's web. The strands which look so lacelike and fragile are really unbelievably strong. If one touches the web gently, it will not break, but the vibration of that touch reaches throughout the entire web and gently rocks the spider. The English poet John Dryden, writing in the seventeenth century, also used this startling parallel. In his play *Marriage à la Mode* he wrote:

> Our souls sit close and silently within,
> And their own web from their entrails spin
> And when eyes meet far off, our sense is such
> That, spider-like, we feel the tenderest touch.

This theme is now being echoed and re-echoed by the environmentalists and conservationists. Indeed, as the sea touches and affects everything in our universe, so indeed do we. It is becoming clearer that all things touch all others.

Our loving heavenly Father, creator of the heaven, the earth, the sea, and everything in them, help us to understand that every action of ours affects all others. Give us the wisdom and the strength to always send out positive vibrations. Help us so to join our strength with others in the community of mankind, that the rippling effect of these positive thoughts and good works will make our world a better place; in Jesus' name. Amen.

Through Sunshine
and Turbulence

*Let the sea roar, and all that fills it, let
the fields exult, and everything in it!*
—I Chronicles 16:32

One of the facets of the sea that is so captivating is its power to change its moods so dramatically. Those who bask on summer sands can recall exact moments when the wind changed, and immediately the surface of hitherto calm waters became rippled. Sometimes these previously glassy surfaces developed such powerful waves that the coast guard had to hoist small-craft warnings. The gentle swish of waves flowing onto the sand had changed to a steady pounding as breakers surged emphatically onto the shore.

Phyllis Meras in her book *Martha's Vineyard Journal* wonders which of these two moods of the sea she likes best.

This week I have been watching storm and sun and trying to choose between the two. . . . I begin to think I have put an unanswerable pair of questions to myself. When the northeast wind blew Tuesday, and the sea thrashed and beach grasses were pulled low to the sand—the way a cat's ears are when it goes into narrow places—I was sure I preferred storm wildness to the tranquility of a sunny day. But when morning came, and the sky was a Delft blue dusted with handfuls of clouds, and still, damp drift roads were dappled with light, and the shadows of cornstalks danced on an Indian Hill barn, I was not so sure.

I wonder if the same question was in the mind of Asaph and his brethren, the Old Testament singers who had been appointed by King David to thank and praise God. Did they recall these swift mood changes of the sea when they sang this scripture? On a Holy Land visit, I recall our guide's telling us that changes of weather are spectacularly fast on the Sea of Galilee, the body of water that figures so often in the Scriptures. A rain squall sweeping across Galilee's surface sometimes tosses boats about with abandon and strikes terror into the hearts of fishermen. Christ and his disciples had that experience. We read in Mark 4:37 that "a great storm of wind arose, and the waves beat into the boat, so that the boat was already filling."

Sudden and in fact instantaneous changes can happen on the sea of life also. Sometimes we experience a long period of sameness. We rest in the routine and walk serenely through the days. Then, often very unexpectedly, there comes a rush of activity. It may be calamitous—an illness, a death, the loss of what we thought was a secure job. The change also could be a challenge—a rush of activity because of new orders in one's business, the excitement of a new arrival in the family, or perhaps the stimulation of helping a new organization become a reality.

As we look back we often ask ourselves which we appreciate most, those periods of calm or the times of tumultuous activity. We are probably inclined to look back on the sunny times as the most idyllic periods, but if we are honest with ourselves, we will probably admit the times of intense activity and travail often taught us truths we would never have learned otherwise.

I recall the anguish, soul-searching, and deep spiritual questioning that followed the news of a life-threatening diagnosis for our beloved daughter. Where was God's will in this? Was it all right to pray for the healing of this one child of God? After several weeks of anguished thoughts and prayers, came the words impressed upon my mind from a source beyond myself: "Christ healed the sick." A load lifted from my mind and heart as I realized he doesn't will sickness but wishes health for each one of his children. It is up to us to pray as well as to work for health, both for individuals and for all mankind. Others might point to similar incidents when, because of stark challenge or deep trouble, they reached spiritual levels not known before. So perhaps the message to be learned from this facet of the sea is that there can be no preference for sunny times over roaring turbulence. Both are in God's plan for his children, and strength will be given to meet and appreciate both.

Our great and glorious heavenly Father, who at one time makes the sea to roar and at another causeth the fields to exult in sunshine, help us to live prayerfully through each of those phases of our life. Grant us the knowledge that strength and power will be available from thee to meet these times and that praising and thanking thee throughout all our days will be the surest way to find victory; in Jesus' name. Amen.

The Greater Call to Love

*So God created the great sea monsters
and every living creature that moves,
with which the waters swarm, according to their kinds.*
—Genesis 1:21*a*

Those who bathe in the ocean, disturbing schools of tiny fish, and those who snorkel and deep-sea dive do not have to be told about the multitudes of creatures that inhabit the seas. Neither do fisher folk who have been feeding on the wealth of the sea since before recorded time began. There is seemingly an unlimited supply of God's creatures inhabiting the land of Poseidon.

Speculation about these creatures and comparisons to the life of mankind have always been rampant. One of the most philosophical books on the subject is *La Mer,* written in 1861 by Jules Michelet, French historian. He writes that the ocean is

a hundred times, a thousand times richer, and more rapidly fecund than the earth. . . . Her sole obstacle is the rapidity of her births; her inferiority appears in the difficulty, which, so rich in generation, she finds in organizing Love. It is melancholy to reflect that the myriads upon myriads of the inhabitants of the sea have only a vague, elementary and imperfect Love. Those vast tribes that, each in its turn, ascend and go in pilgrimage towards pleasure and light, give in floods the best of themselves, their very life to blind and unknown chance. They love, and they will never know the beloved creature in which their dream, their desire was incarnated; they produce multitudes but never know their posterity.

It is true that a few species who lie in the sea do approach love in a human manner. They mate and remain true to their loved ones. For the most part, however, these creatures that inhabit the sea cannot know the unlimited, unselfish love that is a possibility for humans. Like Michelet, we can feel melancholy because these sea creatures have not the capacity to feel and to love as we do. On the other hand, we can also rejoice in the chance we have been given to offer and receive love. We can resolve that we will let no chance go by to exercise this privilege which is at the very heart of our life as humans.

This thought is surely reinforced in the Scriptures by the number of times we are urged to love one another. In Leviticus 19 the Lord said to Moses, "You shall love your neighbor as yourself," and "The stranger who sojourns with you shall be to you as the native among you, and you shall love him as yourself" (vv. 18, 34). Jesus gave this same message in the New Testament when he said, "You shall love Thy neighbor as yourself," and also "Honor thy father and thy mother."

When we wade in shallow water and watch the tiny fish darting to and fro, and when we visit aquariums to see the larger denizens of the deep, we can recall that God's charge to us is more than it is to these creatures of the sea, and we can renew our determination to fulfill more adequately the destiny that is ours.

Perhaps it was a similar thought that prompted an unknown poet to say:

Wisdom—
                    is as vast and ageless as the sea–
            but Love
            and beauty   reach
            beyond its farthest shores.

Our heavenly Father, who has made the innumerable living things in the sea, help us to determine to follow the higher call you have given to humans. Give us the wisdom and will to understand our neighbors and also the strangers we meet. Help us also not to neglect our families. Enable us to always offer a helping hand to others whom we must love as much as we love ourselves; in Jesus' name. Amen.

Hidden Resources

To me, though I am the very least of all the saints, this grace was given, . . . to make all men see what is the plan of the mystery hidden for ages in God who created all things.
—Ephesians 3:8a-9

Often as I sit by the seaside I pick up handfuls of sand and let the tiny grains run through my fingers and marvel at their quantity. Uncountable miles of sand, varying from pale white to jet black, edge this ocean, and if the miles are innumerable, the quantity of grains is mind boggling. Yet this is only a portion of the sand base that extends onto the floor of the sea itself. From these thoughts it is natural to think of the sea and to wonder about the multiplicity of its hidden resources.

Harvard professor Richard G. Darman, vice-president of the 1977 U.S. delegation to the U.N. Conference on the Law of the Sea, is in a position to know about the hidden reserves of the sea. Recently he noted:

The Oceans are not merely a historic source of life and romantic undertaking. They remain literally vital to human existence and a source of exciting promise. They provide major portions of the world's protein, oil, and gas supplies, and are of increasing importance to the expanding global food and energy demands.

They enable efficient expansion of international trade through economical commercial transportation. They permit efficient global information exchange via undersea cable communication. On their sea beds rest vast quantities of hard minerals essential to industrial development. Their ecology influences patterns of weather, the quality of the atmosphere, indeed the basic global environmental balance.

Grains of sand, then, are only tiny symbols of the resources hidden in the sea.

Isn't this somewhat like the hidden resources of our own inner sea? Scientists say most folks are using only a portion of their capabilities, that the brain could be stimulated to produce much greater thought power. Most of our innate abilities are lying untouched, unused.

In like manner our spiritual resources too are largely untapped, lying fallow within us. This is why mystics have appeared in each generation to urge us to set aside time for a quiet waiting upon the Lord. Elizabeth O'Connor, one of our modern mystics who speaks with an authentic voice, makes a plea for such quiet in her book *Journey Inward, Journey Outward:* "I am not practised in placing my life beside quiet waters where the spirit of God can brood upon it. The still waters are for moments of crisis. The small happenings I respond to by the counsel of men conformed to the world, but I am acquainted with another world enough to be uneasy."

E. Stanley Jones, the great missionary and mystic of this past generation, knew the value of a time apart. Wherever he was and however busy he might have been he always set time aside for his "listening post." No wonder he accomplished so much in a lifetime.

Ms. O'Connor acknowledges the difference between her writing done in the ordinary way and when a creative power wells up from within. Of the latter she says, "There is a book which can come out of the depths of one's self, so that the ordinary is transcended and one is surrendered to the creative force that moves through all things."

Surely the uncountable grains of sand and the great, hidden riches of the sea can remind us of the unlimited resources within ourselves. These might have been in the mind of the apostle Paul in today's scripture. As we listen to the Divine and as we work to the best of our abilities we will be reaching some of those hidden resources. Then, along with Ms. O'Connor, we will find "the place that was prepared for us when the foundations of our lives were laid."

Creator God, remind us by inner promptings that we must set aside time for thee. Encourage us to spend our working hours well. Help us to unlock the hidden resources within our soul; in Jesus' name. Amen.

Food from the Sea

And God said, "Let the waters bring forth swarms of living creatures." . . . And God blessed them, saying "Be fruitful and multiply and fill the waters in the seas."
—Genesis 1:20a, 22a

The ocean is becoming increasingly more important in the lives of all people even though many may never have seen it. Those who live on the great inland plains or on the slopes of mountains far from seashore are still in need of all that the ocean can supply. In these days of dwindling land resources the sea is becoming more important as a source of food, energy, and minerals.

Scientists are particularly challenged right now to find additional food supplies, since the rapidly increasing population of the planet has outstripped the traditional forms of food production like gardening, fishing, and hunting. Because the land is being gradually covered by people the sea is the obvious place to look. A recent issue of *Saturday Review,* featuring the theme oceans, confirms this. John Ryther, an oceanographer at Woods Hole Oceanographic Institution, is quoted as saying, "We can catch only about 60 million tons of food from the sea, but we can grow some 100 million tons with simple technology and a worldwide program of aquaculture." Author Susan Schiefelbein calls the sea "a vast farmland. . . . Farming fish seems more promising than farming cattle, for properly managed, an acre of water can produce ten times as much as an acre of pastureland."

There are a few notable pilot projects now in operation. Dr. Howard Wilcox of the Naval Undersea Center in San Diego is researching a fast-growing kelp that doesn't age, that replaces its fronds as they are picked, and that reproduces its weight every six months. Kelp supplies food and energy since it can be converted into methane gas. Another unusual "farm" is found in Mexico where experiments indicate two thousand to three thousand pounds of shrimps can eventually be harvested yearly from one acre of water.

Scientists warn, however, that we mustn't allow the oceans to become a "global garbage dump" or allow giant corporations to plunder the oceans' resources or this abundance will not be available to mankind.

As we gaze across this limitless ocean expanse we wonder if our God had humans of the twentieth century in mind when he said long ago to sea creatures, "Be fruitful and multiply and fill the waters of the seas." These creatures have done their part, for the sea literally teems with life. Now it is up to us to do our part by protecting and developing this eternal and benevolent resource.

One of the late Robert Kennedy's favorite verses according to his biographer Arthur Schlesinger, Jr., in *Robert Kennedy and His Times,* came from Alfred Lord Tennyson's epic *Ulysses.*

> The lights begin to twinkle from the rocks:
> The long day wanes: the slow moon climbs: the deep
> Moans round with many voices. Come, my friends,
> 'Tis not too late to seek a newer world.

No, it's not yet too late to turn to the age-old ocean and seek its newer world.

Our gracious heavenly Father, who knowest our needs before we ourselves are aware of them, we thank you for the bountiful supply of food you have placed in the sea. Give us the wisdom and the commitment to develop these resources in the best possible way and to make this manna from the sea available to all mankind; in Jesus' name. Amen.

Rest and Renewal

*That same day Jesus went out of the
house and sat beside the sea.*
—Matthew 13:1

According to the Bible, Jesus had been very busy this day healing and teaching. Crowds followed him as if drawn by a magnet, and his emotional and physical energy had been depleted in ministering to them. The opposition from religious leaders was mounting. It was a time of tension for our Lord. So he slipped out of the house to seek rest and renewal by the quiet sea. Our Lord's humanness was very much evident here, for work-wearied mankind has ever sought relaxation and refreshment by waterways, and he was no exception.

To be sure, the sea Jesus sought was not the great sea that surrounds the earth. It was the Sea of Galilee which is quite small as seas go. The Great Lakes of America are much larger. Galilee is an enlargement of the Jordan River and measures thirteen miles in length and six miles in width. It is a gem of a tiny sea, though, as the blue skies are reflected in its clear, cool water and as graceful boats ply its surface. The water teems with fish, and a few picturesque villages dot its shores.

One unknown poet, perhaps after meditating on this very Bible verse, wrote:

Clear silver water in a cup of gold,
It shines—his lake—the sea of Galilee—
The waves he loved, the waves that kissed his feet
So many blessed days, O happy waves!
Oh, little silvery happy sea.

We can empathize with Jesus. We too experience pressures, tensions, and a feeling of having too much work to do. When we feel that our concerns are too much to bear, we too can escape to the seaside (or perhaps a lake or a stream if we are not close to the ocean).

Horace Sutton, well-known travel writer, expressed this beautifully when he wrote:

It took me a long time to learn from the sea. . . . Not until I spent summer months in Hawaii, and eventually came to live there for a time, did I understand about the sea—how you come to its edge with your cares, and walk along its fringes, and let it lift them all away from you, relegating to manageable perspective what had loomed so large, diminishing small worries instantly with the timeless lapping at the shore.

Is it easier for the spirit of God to sweep through us at the seaside? Who can really say? We cannot announce this positively, but we can point out that exposure to the sea's invigorating water brings us closer to nature and thus to its creator. The fresh breezes of God's spirit seem closer here. As the wind from the sea or lake invigorates and cleanses us, so the spirit of God breaks in upon us. A dull careworn life comes alive with new dreams, fresh thoughts, renewed aims. There is no need to feel stale and discouraged, the breezes seem to say. "God is near. The very air is charged with His spirit. Let it sweep through you."

"We need times set apart—seaside experiences," declared C. Willard Fetter in a sermon entitled "Seaside Reflections," "for refreshment and enlargement and renewal, but they are not ends in themselves. They are periods when our batteries are recharged so we can face the tasks and responsibilities of our common life with new vigor . . . to get back to the job of working for the welfare of our fellow men."

This is of course what Jesus did, and so must we. These seaside moments will be a time to treasure and remember as we head back into the hectic world again.

Our heavenly Father, thank you for moments by the sea. May they refresh and renew us for life's continuing journey. When we are again enveloped in our busy days, may we carry a memory of the strength we received by the seashore; in Jesus' name. Amen.

Limitless Horizons

He shall command peace to the nations;
his dominion shall be from sea to sea,
and from the River to the ends of the earth.
                                                    —Zechariah 9:10b

Almost every day we have occasion to drive along the shore by cresent-shaped Craigville Beach. Without fail we exclaim over the breadth of the horizon as it stretches limitlessly before us. Sometimes the horizon is hardly discernible because the grayness of sky and of sea blend into each other. At other times the abrupt meeting of the brilliant blue of the atmosphere and the deeper green of the ocean causes the horizon almost to flaunt itself. Always, though, whatever the weather and color, we are caught by the unlimited expanse. It seems to beckon us to other places in distant lands.

Jesus, we are sure, felt this pull of the horizon. Although we know from scripture that he loved the hills, it is obvious that at times he craved the more expansive view that is generated by the sea's horizon. As he sat there no doubt his thoughts went far beyond ours. Perhaps he was musing on today's scripture wherein an Old Testament prophet predicted the coming of the Messiah and hinted that someday the horizon would be lifted to reveal an expanse we cannot even imagine.

I have always been fascinated by horizons, especially those in our personal lives. How far we see ahead in faith is totally determined by us. I believe we make our own horizon. There is a natural tendency among us beginning in babyhood to consider ourselves the center of the universe with all else revolving around us. As we grow, our horizons extend. True maturity comes when we realize that God is at the center of our universe and that we revolve around him. Furthermore, God's children of every race and nation are our neighbors, and our horizons include them.

Jesus never traveled far in this world. His physical world consisted only of Bethlehem, Nazareth, Jerusalem, and nearby villages. Yet his horizon was unlimited. "Go ye into all the world and make disciples of all nations," he said. Jesus constantly held up distant horizons to all people.

Methodist bishop William A. Quale was noted for doing the same. In a book entitled *Spires of the Spirit,* Dr. Frederick Brown Harris recounted an incident when Bishop Quale was conversing with a group of men on a train. Since he did not have on his clerical collar these new acquaintances did not know of his life's work. They thought he was a salesman. One asked, "What is your line?" The bishop replied, "Horizons." He couldn't have used a better word, noted Brown, for wherever he went he "extended the range of what men and women saw."

My clergyman husband loves to tell the story of a stranger who approached three men who were hard at work cutting stone in a quarry. "What are you doing?" the stranger asked. "Cutting stone," replied the first. "Working for a paycheck," said the second. The third straightened up and with a proud gleam in his eye responded, "Cutting stone blocks for a cathedral to the glory of God and the service of man."

Like the third man, sometimes we must look far beyond our daily tasks and know that what we are doing is a small but vital part of God's plan, a plan that extends far beyond our limited horizons.

Our heavenly Father, whose horizon encompasses all things, help us to lift our finite eyes to yours. Remind us as we gaze at the physical horizon that our spiritual one can be limitless if we but make it so. Help us to do all in our power to extend our own horizon and that of others; in Jesus' name. Amen.

A Sea Uncontrollable

For thus says the Lord of hosts: Once again, in a little while, I will shake the heavens and the earth and the sea and the dry land.

—Haggai 2:6

Part of the fascination of the sea is its uncontrollableness. No matter how much knowledge mankind absorbs, no matter how intricate his inventions, he still cannot master the sea. As Natalie Babbitt has written in the prologue to her book *The Eyes of the Amaryllis,*

The sea can swallow ships, and it can spit out whales upon the beach like watermelon seeds. It will take what it wants and it will keep what it has taken, and you may not take away from it what it does not wish to give. Listen. No matter how old you grow or how important on land, no matter how powerful or beautiful or rich, the sea does not care a straw for you. That frail grip you keep on the wisp of life that holds you upright—the sea can turn it loose in an instant.

We were starkly reminded of this one recent autumn. The *Queen Elizabeth* is one of the greatest of modern ships. It is a veritable floating city with shops, restaurants, movie houses, and thousands of passengers. It is, according to the public-relations releases, an air-conditioned luxury liner 963 feet long and 105 feet wide. It would seemingly be rocklike in any storm. Yet on a recent trip the great ship encountered a major hurricane with "Force 12" winds, the maximum on the Beaufort scale. The furious storm picked up the 66,851-ton ship and tossed it about like a matchstick. Though the captain insisted that at no time was it in danger, it is a fact that services were greatly curtailed, passengers knocked about, and the ship was twenty-seven hours late in making port. No matter that a horde of "beautiful people" were aboard. The sea has the final say. As Haggai the prophet said when speaking the words the Lord put in his mouth, "I will shake the heavens and the earth and the sea." At times he literally does.

The sea of life is sometimes as uncontrollable. Most of our days are ordinary and serene, filled with a round of duties and simple pleasures. But once in a while life hands us a buffeting blow, and the storm of life rages around us. Our safe anchorage is gone. We are pulled loose and cast adrift in a sea of worry.

Fortunately God has not left us without spiritual anchors. If we have lived close to him, we have gradually become aware that there is a world beyond this which is invisible to the normal senses. It is a world we are led into by faith. The first tenuous steps into this spiritual world gradually become firmer as by prayer, meditation, and Bible-reading we grow in the knowledge of it.

Author Thomas Merton, Trappist monk extraordinary, was

well aware of this when he wrote in his book, *The Christian Response:*

As man's mastery over nature accelerates by virtue of his expanding scientific and technological knowledge, his mastery over the interior universe of his own personality diminishes.[He cautions:] When man forsakes the spirit, he loses all else in his wake. . . . Let me hasten to add, however, that we not only do not have the right to bridle the staggering progress made in modern times but we have an urgent obligation to work at the task rather than run from it. Let us not forget, however, that we will have laboured in vain if we do not at the same time strive to make man aware that he possesses an immortal spirit.

The best way to face life, he seems to say, is with one foot in this world and the other foot in the next. A retired minister in his eighties testified vividly to this when he remarked to a group of friends: "The older we grow, the more my wife and I cherish our times of meditation and prayer. It almost seems as if we are gradually relinquishing this world and strengthening the life that is to flourish after death."

Perhaps the mighty storms that shake the ocean are meant to remind us that the physical world is a tenuous thing, but the undergirding life of the spirit can carry us through any crisis and into the life everlasting.

Our heavenly Father, creator of worlds known and unknown, give us the wisdom to see that our lives are twofold—both physical and spiritual. Help us to nourish both, and guide us into a firmer relationship with thee; in Jesus' name. Amen.

God's Guidance

*And he will guide them to springs of
living water.*
—Revelation 7:17*b*

A visitor to the edge of the sea is fascinated by the gulls that swoop and dip above the water searching for succulent morsels and by the bands of tiny sandpipers who with flying feet deftly skirt the edges of the waves. Reflection on these birds brings to mind other sea creatures that seem to know what they are doing and where they are going. What gives them their guidance?

In a book about a fisherman in Chatham, Massachusetts, called *One Man and His Sea,* Gordon Smith has the same wonderment.

Gulls and terns roam air currents in storms and fogs and seem to know where they are headed. Fishes and creatures of the oceans seem to know something about their elevations and their whereabouts in migrations. Lobsters seem to have senses that do not parallel those of man's and man seems at a loss to understand them because he has not those senses to understand them with.

What is more thrilling than the stirring sounds and sight of a flock of Canadian geese rising majestically from an inlet or a pond? They seem to fly as if on a mission. We marvel at their obvious purposeful flight, their precise V formation. What radar of nature guides them? What do they know that we do not? How can we learn from them?

Could it be that we have withdrawn from nature to such an extent that we no longer truly empathize with our fellow creatures? Have urban centers of concrete and carefully manicured subdivisions created such barriers between us and

44

animals, birds, and fish that we no longer observe and learn from them?

Many a time humans have longed to be as sure of themselves as geese are in flight, as unerring in purpose as the tiny sandpipers. It would be such a comfort, we think, to know where we are going and why, to have no anxious moments of choice when two paths lie ahead. To be sure of our decisions would be such a relief. Is this perhaps why many folks, young and old, are drawn to cults, to the Eastern religions, and to those Western religions in which beliefs are solid and unchanging and where individual thinking is discouraged? I can imagine the relief this must be to over-anxious folks who are unable to cope with an increasingly hectic world.

But we must remember as we watch the gulls and the sandpipers and think of those other purposeful creatures in God's world that we have been offered help and guidance.

"Let not your heart be troubled," said Christ and later added, "When the Spirit of Truth comes he will guide you into all truth." The psalmist also brought this message from God: "I will instruct you and teach you the way you should go. I will counsel you with my eye upon you." Isaiah affirmed it too, saying, "And the Lord will guide you continually."

If these biblical promises are true, and I firmly believe they are, then it is up to us to take time from our busy schedules to listen for this guidance and to allow the Spirit of Truth to illumine our paths. Taking regular moments for silent meditation is one way to lock into our spiritual radar. John Sherrill, who has recently authored a moving book entitled *My Friend the Bible,* has pointed out another way. He witnesses glowingly to the part Bible reading can play in guidance. Using the Episcopal Church Lectionary, he delved deeper into the Bible and found that portions seemed mysteriously activated, "charged with power intended just for my right-now situation." "Could it be," he asks, "that Jesus is still opening the scriptures to us? Individually? Now? As we face problems?" His continued immersion in the Bible confirmed these questions; so Bible readings too can help keep us on course.

I can only conclude that humans as well as nature's creatures have been offered the opportunity of purposeful and guided living and that, as our verse for today affirms, he will guide us to these springs of living water if we do our part.

Creator of the natural world as well as the human, thank you for the lessons revealed to us by gulls, terns, sandpipers, lobsters, and Canadian geese. Guide us as you do them in all our paths, and help us always to remain in close touch with thee; in Jesus' name. Amen.

Spiritual Sonar

Yet a little while, and the world will see me no more, but you will see me; because I live, you will live also. In that day you will know that I am in my Father, and you in me, and I in you.
—John 14:19-20

Dolphins are playful creatures that gambol and cavort in offshore waters, delighting seagoing travelers. It is generally less known that these appealing mammals have cousins who live in freshwater and occasionally become friendly with humans.

Jean Little, writing recently in the *Christian Science*

Monitor, told of the dolphins that lived near her family in the Guiana Highlands. As the Littles arrived at their new home, their guide pointed out the dark shapes gliding underneath their dugout. "Boutos," he said, giving them the local name. Though the guide assured the Littles the boutos were friendly, months later they were still only dark shapes in the water, swimming in and out of the leaf-shaped pool that was their home. Jean Little's family lived near the boutos for a full year before the shy mammals decided these humans were not to be feared. Finally, one happy day, the boutos surfaced, showing their friendliness by a conspicuous trailing of surface water and speaking in teasing snorts. Their conversation, she reports, is "eerily human, rather like someone fallen asleep in the bathtub and coming awake gasping in surprise."

Dolphins, which are some of the earth's most venerable creatures, extend back in time about 30 million years. They have a remarkably acute and sensitive ability to "see" by hearing. Though living in water, they seem to know what happens on land. Theirs is a balanced and happy life. They never feed to depletion or increase too rapidly, we are told.

Humans, and especially scientists, are becoming increasingly aware of the dolphins, their abilities, and their friendliness, realizing they have much to teach us. Dolphins are now being trained to assist in underwater experiments. They help divers to attach ropes to underwater objects, for example. Their sonar ability is being studied and has already been the basis for sonar equipment on ships. This ability to communicate without words is becoming increasingly important to humans as we become closer allied to the mysterious and miraculous universe through experiments in extrasensory perception (ESP). The longer we live, the more we realize that the world of senses is only a front for a deeper level of reality.

Eda LeShan, writing in *Woman's Day* on ESP, tells of her

48

husband Lawrence's investigations and developing theories in this field.

The more Larry studied the experiences of psychics, the more convinced he became that we limit ourselves as human beings because we are afraid to experience this other, more expansive level of reality in which we are so powerfully joined to one another.

We need of course to live in the world of our senses, there is no other way to cross a street safely, cook our food, read a map, get to our jobs on time. But there is more to being human, and we've barely begun to acknowledge how desperately we need the "world of the One."

Jesus knew this of course and lived with part of himself in the world of reality and part in the realm of the Spirit—one foot here and one in heaven. He calls us to do the same, assuring us of this other world in today's scripture.

Perhaps the dolphins have been placed in this world to remind us that though we must live in the real world and be happy in it, we must not forget that it is possible to be aware of something else beyond.

Infinite Creator, our thanks for these creatures of the water world who are sensitive to those of us who are outside their milieu. May we similarly be as conscious of a spiritual existence around us while yet we live in the world of the senses; in Jesus' name. Amen.

Moving Water

Worship him who made heaven and earth, the sea and the fountains of water.
—Revelation 14:7*b*

Moving water has always fascinated people. Is it because the action is so incessant as in the continuous motion of the sea? But the ocean does not have the only moving water.

There is a spectacular sight in Geneva, Switzerland, where a fountain rises 400 feet above Lac Leman (Lake Geneva). Seen by daylight the majestic upward thrust of the world's tallest water fountain is impressive. Seen at night when lighted by multicolored floodlights, it is a fairyland object. This *jet d'eau*, with output of 110 gallons per second, is famous the world over.

David von Schlegell, artist and Yale professor, was also fascinated by liquid movement. When chosen to create a sculpture for a huge, dark, dead space at the Byrne Green Federal Courthouse in Philadelphia, he noted, "Two forms of active water have always seemed beautiful to me: the twisting bow wave of a ship and the transparent curved flow over a dam." Using these forms he designed a fountain that dramatically activated a dead spot. He titled the sculpture *The Voyage of Ulysses* because it was a "metaphor for the dimly perceived but grand emotions and events from the deep past providing resonance to our concept of time."

Whether it be the hardly perceived recollection of things past known to us only through ancestral memory or whether it is the thrilling sense of thrust of the Geneva fountain, it is true that moving water evokes a response from us—and we haven't yet mentioned waterfalls which also bring a lift to the heart.

We don't know what was in the mind of the writer of Revelation when he referred to fountains of water. He may have meant waterspouts, which are mighty powerful and much to be feared by seagoing travelers. We do know he felt moving water was important, mentioning it in the same sentence as he does the heavens, the earth, and the sea.

I like to think moving water is a symbol for pressing forward. It is a reminder that all life flows continuously through time. If we don't make our life grow and advance, it is as if we retreat. There is no standing still in the moving flow of time. This concept has taken root more surely in recent years. As there are more and more elderly and the life-span has been prolonged, there has been an increasing emphasis on second careers and meaningful hobbies in retirement. Schools are establishing continuing-education programs. Volunteer jobs are encouraged.

Is there a message here for the churches? Why do so many cease the educational programs at the high school level? Don't we need to continue our spiritual growth, our reach toward true maturity all through our days? Aren't we called constantly to be pilgrims throughout our earthly years?

Perhaps the magnificent soaring water, like the ceaseless movement of the sea, is to be a constant reminder that we are to move ever onward, never treading water in the pathway of life.

Father of worlds we cannot see as well as the world we can see, help us to be reminded by the mighty thrust of moving water that we must constantly press onward in our search for thee. Give us the will to persevere so that our roots may grow sturdier, our fruits more visible, and our faith much greater as the years roll on; in Jesus' name. Amen.

Fulfilling a Mission

A garden fountain, a well of living water,
and flowing streams from Lebanon.
—Song of Solomon 4:15

There is a broad river emptying into Nantucket Sound, which could tell an ancient story if it could speak. I think of that long-ago era every time I drive across the substantial bridge over Bass River. Native Americans lived along these riverbanks. In summer they gathered shellfish and walked the sandy shores at its mouth as we do today. Some say Lief Ericson's dragon-prowed ship nosed carefully up the river's length to moor in what we call Follins Pond about the year A.D. 1000. There are vintage mooring holes at its rocky edge that seem to substantiate this claim.

Bass River tells a modern story too. Any pleasant day it is filled with boats of all sizes and descriptions. Some bear day sailors on excursions. Others carry fishermen on their daily jobs. More casual fishermen hold fishing poles over the bridge rail seeking to catch their dinner. Still other folks scour the sands at the river's mouth seeking treasures tossed up by the sea or trudge along its sandy edge on exhilarating walks.

I like to view the river by leaning over the bridge's side and peering into its depths. One can soon sense there is more activity here than meets the casual eye. There is unceasing noise—gurgling, rushing, murmuring, slapping sounds. Underneath surface currents are countercurrents swirling and eddying. Sometimes the major current is flowing seaward. Then, when the tide turns, it flows inland again. Always, however, the river is fulfilling its ancient mission, bringing water from inland regions to the sea.

This river is unlike the streams of Lebanon in our

51

scripture, which brings crystal-clear water from snowcapped mountains to the sea. Our river's mission is just as important, however, as it drains water from the pine-covered highlands and guides it gently seaward. The stream, whether in Viking days or now, is fulfilling its unique mission, and I must do the same.

Why am I here but to fulfill the destiny that became mine when I was born? It is up to me, then, to know myself better, to discover my talents and special abilities. I must seek next to develop and train them so they flower into what God meant them to be.

I catch my breath as I glimpse a faraway vision of what the world might be like if every soul flowered perfectly into what he or she was designed to become and so form an interlocking pattern in which each ministering to others makes a perfect whole.

A passing motorboat headed toward the open sea abruptly breaks my reverie and brings me back from a world that someday might be. No matter that human frailty stops this perfect world from happening. Is that any reason we shouldn't pledge to do our part?

I turn away, hoping to look again into my own heart, and find ways of releasing the gifts deep within me. One part of me groans, for it seems an impossible task. I take comfort in the words of Rainer Maria Rilke:

Be patient toward all that is involved in your heart. . . . Try to love the questions themselves like locked rooms and like books that are written in a very foreign tongue. Do not seek the answers. . . . Live the questions now. Perhaps you will then gradually, without noticing it live along some distant day into the answer.

I say good-bye for a while to my river, vowing to carry its message safely wrapped in my heart.

Almighty God, as this river constantly fulfills the mission you have given it from the beginning of creation, may I too find the talents buried deep within me and carry out the plans you have set for me from my beginnings; in Jesus' name. Amen.

Obedience to Our Natural Gifts

But let justice roll down like waters,
and righteousness like an
everflowing stream.
—Amos 5:24

I am irresistibly drawn to the mouth of rivers, streams, and creeks that carry the perpetual flow of inland water into the infinite maw of the sea. Today I am walking ankle deep in the gravelly bed of Hall Creek on Cape Cod watching the eddies swirl like miniature whirlpools as the fresh water meets the salt.

Here the fresh water bumps into a sandbar that partially closes the mouth of the creek. Undaunted, the current beats against the barrier. Turning aside, it runs along the sandbar for a time until the sand ceases and it can again turn seaward.

Upstream a stone bars another current, abruptly turning it back whence it came. The obstruction baffles the water only temporarily, however. Soon it turns and tries again. This time it safely navigates the channel, dancing past the unyielding rock in triumph. Running, dancing, leaping, pushing, and drifting, it inevitably reaches the sea, obeying the orders given to it before the beginning of time.

As I gaze up the creek I can see many such currents moving in small swirling patterns. Though differing from one another, they are still part of one whole motion. Their common objective is being accomplished in many subtle forms.

I am struck by how similar this is to humanity, where much seemingly separate activity is actually a part of one great whole. Aren't we in the animate world as destined for certain pathways as are objects in the inanimate world? Aren't we, like dancing streams, happiest when we find out what our own particular pathways are, then follow where they lead?

Sometimes we wonder what God's will is for us, what path he wishes us to take. Yet if we examine our natural abilities, our inclinations, our expertise, we usually find that our pathway is linked to these. Why else would we be given these abilities? Jesus indicated such in the story of the talents. That parable is not only about money, it is also about our gifts. As Elizabeth O'Connor says in *The Eighth Day of Creation,* we perceive God's will when "we discern our gifts. . . . Our gifts are on loan. We are responsible for spending them in the world and we will be held accountable." But suppose we dance happily along doing what we love best and we come across a roadblock? A job ends, perhaps, or an accident happens. Then we can recall the lesson of the water that met a rock that barred the path of the water's current. Like the adjustable water, we can back away, and try another path. Many times these seeming disappointments become stepping-stones to new opportunities. If we persevere, we find ourselves dancing along again on our ever-rolling stream, leaping, running, and perhaps drifting briefly as we rest before continuing on our path. Like the currents in the stream, we will inevitably reach our goal by obediently following our natural gifts. Obedience and surrender to our gifts are really obedience and surrender to God. No doubt it will be a lifetime of struggle, surrender, and obedience. Yet it will probably not seem like a struggle, for we will be in the place we are meant to be, doing what God commands.

God of creativity, increase in us the knowledge of our own creative gifts. Help us to develop and follow them through out our life so that we may better serve thee; in Jesus' name. Amen.

Open to the Flow

He makes his wind blow, and the waters flow.
—Psalm 147:18*b*

Although I have often observed that water is constantly in motion, I had not thought until recently how necessary this motion is to the water. Apparently the psalmist noted this, for he saw that waters flow to a Divine command. They cease flowing at their peril. If ever water is caught in a pool with no way to move on, it becomes stagnant—good neither for man nor beast.

An oft told example of this is the contrast between the Sea of Galilee and the Dead Sea in the Holy Land. The Sea of Galilee welcomes water from the surrounding hills, then sends it along down the Jordan River. Both the sea itself and the water that gurgles from it are swift-flowing and healthy. I have waded at that point; so I know.

In contrast, the Dead Sea welcomes the healthy waters of the Jordan but keeps them to itself. Since there is no outlet, the water becomes stagnant, salty, and unhealthy for man and fish. I recall a fellow traveler from Utah rushing to its shore to see if it were saltier than the Great Salt Lake. Ruefully he decided it is. We could tell by looking that it is not exactly a mecca for fishermen.

The difference between the two bodies of water is in their motion, or flow, and this is also true in our life. As Klemens Tilmann writes in his book *The Practice of Meditation:* "Since his exaltation, Christ has not given even a spoonful of soup to any poor person apart from us. We are the channels through which his love flows from the source into the world." As God's only channels, how important it is that we open our life to the motion and flow of his Spirit. The flow must be from him and to others.

An awesome thought, this. If our life takes but does not give, then the overflowing water of Christ's love is stopped up within us, becoming stagnant and unhealthy. Not only does it do no good to our own personality, but, even worse, the folks who were meant to be reached and touched with this Divine love never receive it.

How can we show this love in our place on earth in this moment in time? "We can show it in our faces," says Tilmann,

our eyes, the palms of our hands, our mouths with a friendly helpful word or good advice. . . . In serving others and expressing our love for them, we experience God's love flowing through us. . . . This is the action of the Holy Spirit in us, the Spirit of Christ . . . the love of God flowing from this source, through us . . . into the world.

As we watch the flowing water in stream, river, or ocean, we can imagine God's spirit of love flowing from the divine source through our body, into our hands, our face, our feet, then flowing out to others.

The poet Annie Johnson Flint expressed it clearly when she wrote:

Christ has no hands but our hands
To do His work today,
He has no feet but our feet
To lead man in His way.

Then she asks penetratingly:

What if our hands are busy
With other work than His?

O Divine Source of All Things, we open our hearts to thy spirit. Let it flow unceasingly like water through us to others. May we always remember that it is our duty and joy to keep a moving channel of thy love within us in order to refresh those with whom we come in contact; in Jesus' name. Amen.

Treasures of the Sea

The sea is his, for he made it;
for his hands formed the dry land.
—Psalm 95:5

Recently I watched an amazing television documentary from the Nova series that showed industrial conglomerates testing machines to be used in recovering tiny black nodules from the ocean floor. Entitled *Cashing In on the Ocean*, the engrossing film depicted the worldwide contest to tap the vast mineral treasures lying on the seabed. Five consortia have already spent 150 million dollars searching this undersea world, and the treasure hunt is only just beginning. One consortium has even staked out a claim off the islands of Hawaii. It is not clear how binding a seabed claim is. This is yet to be determined by the 140 nations struggling to write a treaty governing the use of the world's oceans.

One editorial writer warned: "The seabed is a vast treasure house of valuable deposits of nickel, copper, cobalt, manganese, and perhaps gold. The industrial nations hold the key to unlocking these treasures, but the Third World nations feel these treasures are for the good of all, not just the industrial nations." So the heated debate continues endlessly even as the consortia perfect their equipment and range the seas looking for the areas of richest deposits.

It is difficult to imagine, as I sit here gazing over the surface of an azure ocean, that the deep-sea floor is strewn with these black marblelike nodules. It is much easier to imagine the undulating stems and blossoms of sea anemone or the gentle movement of multicolored fish. Underwater photography has made these scenes familiar, whereas the deep-sea scenes have only begun to appear since tiny submarines have gone to seven-mile depths. There is no doubt, however, that these nodules are there. The first tentative probing with extended rubbery arms and dragging scoops have brought these minerals to the surface.

Thus it is not too soon for all the world's peoples to think about the mining of the sea floor. It is inevitable that these treasures will be brought to the surface from the seamounts and escarpments miles below the surface. To whose benefit will they accrue? The proposal for an international seabed authority seems reasonable; planned controls to benefit both industrial and developing nations are in the right direction.

We must never forget that like the resources of the land which we are beginning only now to protect, these were created for all mankind. As the psalmist reminds us, the Creator fashioned both land and sea. It is inconceivable that they would be for a favored few.

Black Elk, great native American prophet of the Ogalala Sioux who lived in the last century, remembered a time when the emphasis was not on individual ownership of the land.

Once we were happy in our own country and we were seldom hungry, for then the two-leggeds and the four-leggeds lived together like relatives, and there was plenty for them and for us. But the Wasichus [white men] came, and they have made little islands for us and other islands for the four-leggeds, and always these islands are becoming smaller, for around them surges the gnawing flood of the Wasichus.

We mustn't repeat this with the sea and create islands of ownership that benefit the few. If a seabed treaty is completed, global government, the world's peoples, and the message of God the Creator will have triumphed.

God of our globe and universe beyond, we are conscious of the enormous potential in the sea. We ask thy help in moving the minds of men and nations so that this vast treasures will be used for the benefit of all mankind; in Jesus' name. Amen.

Cycles and Circles

And in the morning, a great while before day, he [Jesus] rose and went out to a lonely place, and there he prayed.
—Mark 1:35

Some days when clouds are piled high in the sky like mounds of whipped cream I can discern faint gray ladders mounting from the ocean to the sky. I am reminded of similar scenes when our children were small. God is drawing water up into the clouds to carry it to the thirsty land, we would explain. Their bright eyes searched the mysterious ladders while they wondered how water could travel up into the air when they knew from experience it comes down, not up. A science lesson followed on the cycle and form-change of water as it travels from ocean, to cloud, to rain, to streams, and back to ocean. The water circles through its cycle coming back to its original form, we explained. I am often brought back to that time of wonder when I see ladders connecting ocean and sky in my water view.

Earlier civilizations, including Native American, were well aware of how the cycles and circles occur in nature. Black Elk, the Ogalala Sioux medicine man, said:

You have noticed that everything an Indian does is in a circle, and that is because the Power of the World always works in circles and everything tries to be round. In the old days when we were a strong and happy people, all our power came to us from the sacred hoop of the nation, and so long as the hoop was unbroken, the people flourished. . . . This knowledge came to us from the outer world with our religion. Everything the Power of the World does is in a circle. The sky is round, and I have heard that the earth is round like a ball, and so are all the stars. The wind, in its greatest power whirls. Birds make their nests in circles, for theirs is the same religion as ours. The sun comes forth and goes down in a circle. The moon does the same, and both are round. Even the seasons form a great circle in their changing, and always come back again to where they were.

I wonder if there aren't circles and cycles in our personal life also. Should we also allow time for ladders in our own soul—those times apart when the senses are tranquilized and our spent self is replenished?

Don Gold, writing recently in *Travel and Leisure* magazine on the art of doing nothing, would agree; for he goes on vacation to seek "silence not sloth." Like actors Hume Cronyn and Jessica Tandy who regularly retreat to their secluded Bahama home for replenishing, he seeks the therapeutic silence of solitude. The nineteenth-century Concord sage Henry David Thoreau also would agree, for he noted that in seeming to do nothing, one is doing something extraordinarily good for oneself.

The beach is the perfect place to reflect on cycles and circles. There one can relax on ancient sands, taking comfort in the age-old water cycle that one can see, and refresh that less-visible inner land of our soul. It is at these times we can see with greater clarity where we are and where we are going. We can know that times of activity and accomplishment must be alternated with periods of rest and quiet.

Surely this must have been one of the secrets of Jesus' life. We know from the gospel record that he went apart before daybreak to a lonely place. Cycles and circles properly recognized and appreciated take us back to where we began, refreshed and ready for life's cycles and circles to continue.

Our Father God, who set the cycles of the world in motion, help us to understand the cycles and circles in our own life. Give us the wisdom to fall into this ancient pattern and find refreshment to continue our work for thy kingdom; in Jesus' name. Amen.

Hovering Gulls

Like birds hovering, so the Lord of hosts
will protect Jerusalem.
—Isaiah 31:5a

Sea gulls are ever-present along our shores. They fly lazily overhead, then dive into the sea for food. They hover near people, scavenging from beach picnickers and sailors at sea. They have learned that shellfish dropped from a great height on macadam surfaces crack open, revealing a succulent interior. No dumbbells these!

I like Grace Noel Crowell's description of them in her poem "Sea Gulls Far Inland."

> Strangers to the land, they light
> A quiver of silver, black and white
> To pluck the grain they need for flight.
> Beautiful, tremulous, shimmering things
> Strength of the sea wind in their wings
> Through every motion the sea's voice sings.

There is a certain comfort in having sea gulls gliding above us on this beach. The weather will be good, we know. There is no storm in the offing to cause them to seek shelter. It is a time of peace and quiet.

According to the Scriptures, the protective mantle of God is like the presence of these gulls hovering over us. We know the message was directed particularly to the inhabitants of Jerusalem, but I like to think it can be broadened to include us today. How nice to feel that the presence of God hovers over us as we go about our tasks.

We do not always consciously feel his presence even though in our mind we know God is there. Yet if we feed our soul with thoughts of him, if we develop a habit of flashing brief prayers throughout the day, if we seek fellowship with like-minded souls, and if we are steeped in the Scriptures, we know the consciousness of this hovering spirit of God will grow stronger.

Thomas Kelley, the Quaker mystic, described this growing certainty in his book *Testament of Devotion.*

There is a way of ordering our mental life on more than one level at once. On one level we may be thinking, discussing, seeing, calculating, meeting all the demands of external affairs. But deep within, behind the scenes, at a profounder level, we may also be in prayer and adoration, song and worship, and have a gentle receptiveness to divine breathings.

The secular world values the first level, saying that that is where life is really lived. But those of a religious nature know that "the deep level of divine attendance . . . is where the real business of life is determined." Here one "lives in resources and powers that make individuals radiant and triumphant."

Beautiful, tremulous, shimmering gulls will always remind me that the spirit of God is hovering over each one of us. Their graceful gliding flight is calling us to orient our lives inward, into the secret silence of the soul where we can be more receptive to the Divine breathings.

Our Father, who art closer than breathing, nearer than hands and feet, enable us to persist in thoughts of thee even though we are engrossed with the routine of living. Help us to become ever more conscious of thy presence; in Jesus' name. Amen.

Taproots

Those who stroll the beaches cannot fail to notice the lowly beach grasses that live at the water's edge wherever a rocky shore will permit. These grasses grow in clumps in the sand, where normally one would expect no green things could live. Newcomers often stand in puzzled wonder, marveling at how these grasses can be so strong and sturdy in arid beds of sand.

The secret of the beach grass is in its underground connection. The stiff, pale green stalks topped with tiny seedpods rise from "creeping rhisomes" that extend for many feet underground. One seemingly separate clump is in reality connected with many others. Attached to this strong taproot, the beach grass is anchored firmly in its element. In times of storm it is resilient, lying flat and giving in to the fury of the gale. When the tempest subsides, the beach grass comes erect again, still sturdy and enduring because of its taproot.

Beach grass has an important job to do. It holds sandy dunes in place. When beach grass is destroyed by careless people, the dunes begin to "move." The wind blows the sand unceasingly, and soon the contours of that stretch of beach have changed. Without beach grass and its taproots our ecology is threatened.

Poet Lila Coburn alluded to this in "Tap Roots for Life."

> The feathery dune grass blows in twists and tangles,
> So fragile seeming, winter bleached and thinned,
> And yet it holds by tap roots far below it
> Against the beating rain and icy wind.

I muse on these taproots as I finger the clump of faded green beach grass near my beach blanket this summer day. Aren't we meant to have taproots too? Is God telling us through this lowly beach grass that we must develop deep inner roots in order to weather life's storms? Is he telling us to strengthen our inner resources so that we may be better prepared for life's problems? Was that what the apostle Paul was referring to when he urged the new Christians to be strong in the Lord and in the power of his might?

My mind turns back to moments when people I have known have been buffeted by the storms of life. Some wilted, bewailing their fate. Others, sometimes when it was least expected, met the emotional blows staunchly, standing sturdily erect afterward. Human taproots are important too, I thought.

Our poet believed this also, for she closed with this verse:

> As I watch the weather rough and ravening,
> Like storms of life which will not be cajoled,
> I sense the wisdom in the strength of tap roots,
> For tap roots hold.

Our Divine Creator, who made the lowly beach grass and other growing things along our shores, help us to learn from them. Give us the wisdom, the will, and the commitment to develop our taproots so that in times of trouble we may stand firm; in Jesus' name. Amen.

Crises on Sea and Land

Some went down to the sea in ships,
doing business in the great waters;
they saw the deeds of the Lord,
his wondrous works in the deep.
—Psalm 107:23

Those of us who are shore folk have no idea how magnificent, how terrifying, how awesome it is to sail upon the ocean. This experience is reserved for those who do business in great waters, for sailors who struggle with the sea.

A glimpse of this awesome experience is given to us by Susan Schlee in her book *On Almost Any Wind,* which is a chronicle of the saga of the *Atlantis,* the research vessel that served the Woods Hole Oceanographic Institution for thirty-five years.

Wind and sea increasing to a howling gale, wrote an unsteady hand. . . . The wind was soon exceeding gale force, and seas heavily streaked with foam rose into the gray sky and toppled and crashed around the ship. Above a layer of low ragged clouds, torn from the east, went flying across the sky, and below, the churning crests raced across the sea. Wind shrieked in the rigging, rain drove across the decks, the ship creaked and groaned, waves roared by like express trains, and everything within sight, sound and feeling seemed bent on hurling itself over the edge of the world.

I don't think a landlubber like me would appreciate that experience. Yet humans have sailed the ocean for eons, facing all the terrors it produces. When faced with a shrinking chance of survival, ocean sailors have known how thin the line is between here and eternity. Sometimes I wonder if they haven't been more privileged than those who live on land by experiencing firsthand the Creator's wonders. Does the

67

observation of these wonders of the deep make the sailors more conscious of a guiding hand behind these natural elements?

I suppose these crises on the sea can be likened to the crises we experience on land. I recall a freak cyclone that hit the heart of Massachusetts some two decades ago leveling homes and businesses in its path. Lives were lost. Not long ago a giant earthquake shook the Alaskan coast, turning houses, hotels, and businesses into rubble in just a few terrible moments. I guess we have a share of wonders on land too.

Perhaps the message behind these wonders of sea and land is that we should be prepared for crises wherever they occur. These can be of the natural world or in human relations. Being human is being vulnerable to crises, for they will surely come to all of us. Jesus noted this when he said, "For he [God] makes his sun to rise on the evil and the good, and sends rain on the just and the unjust."

Whether we walk the slanting deck of a ship or whether we travel on solid ground, we must acknowledge that the fury and power of the natural world at times threatens our peace and our serenity. It is at these times that we reach deep into our spiritual resources. We lay hold of the faith that is needed to face these mighty wonders and deal realistically with them.

Our God, who created the natural world and all the wonders therein, help us cope with whatever befalls us. Give us the inner strength to meet the crises of life whenever they come, in Jesus' name. Amen.

Of Dunes and Deserts

*Make straight in the desert a highway
for our God.*
—Isaiah 40:3b

Today I went walking on the dunes that border the sweeping stretch of Cape Cod's outer beach. How wonderful it was to leave the world behind. On one side of me stretched roaring breakers beyond which, if I could have seen it, lay faraway Spain. On the other side, sand dunes covered with pale green beach grass ascended as high as church steeples. The azure of the sky, the beige of the sand, and the aquamarine of the ocean met ahead of me in infinity at the horizon. Nothing man-made could be seen. It was as if I were in the middle of Africa's Sahara Desert or Asia's Gobi Desert. I felt that far removed from civilization.

This was probably the closest I will come to retreating to a desert. I have read of desert retreats, particularly in the Scriptures. Moses was called to guide the wandering Israelites for forty years in the desert. Elijah ran to the desert to find God again. John the Baptist preached in a desert. Jesus went through forty days of fasting and retreat in a desert. Paul withdrew to a desert after his conversion.

As I walked the lonely sands I found it easier to understand why people withdrew to the desert to meditate. There is nothing animate here but myself. I am more conscious of another Presence. There is nothing to distract me from him.

"The desert is the place where God does his thing, prepares us to receive his grace, opens with us a passage," wrote Roy J. Council in the magazine *alive now.* "In the desert the crooked paths are made straight, the high places are brought low, and the rough, uneven spots made smooth. The desert is our mentor or guru. There God gives us a new heart and a new spirit."

69

As I trudged laboriously in the sand, which is not the easiest place to walk, I willed my senses to record these moments. I listen. I look. I hear. I feel. There will be times when I will need to withdraw to a desert place, but I will be far from here. Though I will be gone from these dunes, I want to be able to recall this experience from the depths of memory. Though my desert place may actually be a corner of my living room or the desk in my writing grotto, I will remember this day and my walk in the dunes. I hope this experience will make it easier for me to withdraw into solitude in "a desert place."

As I look back now on my day, I reflect that desert periods are necessary in our life, but I am glad they last for only a little while. Special places of isolation, they are perfect spots for recollection, meditation, and resting in the Infinite. It is here we feel a Presence searching for us. It is here we are alone yet not alone.

But then our desert period ends. When refreshed and renewed, we seem to be propelled by God back into the world. Just as the desert periods in the Bible were preparation for servanthood, so our desert times are preludes to service. The desert is only a stage of a journey. Yet it was good to have retreated to desert dunes for a time.

Our Father, who at times seems so close, help us to carry the memory of our desert experiences back into the world. May we ever be conscious that when work in the world looms larger than it should, the quiet desert places are waiting; in Jesus' name. Amen.

A Great Rain

And in a little while the heavens grew
black with clouds and wind, and there
was a great rain.
                              —I Kings 18:45a

I cannot go to the beach today. The rain is descending in torrents. The wind whips sheets of water horizontally around the house. Millions of raindrops beat relentlessly against my windowpanes. I cannot see the ocean because the rain has drawn a curtain. Puddles are growing along the road and in the gullies. I wander disconsolately through the house. A dip in the cool salt water and a rest in the warm sun are part of my daily summer ritual, and I am lost when they are taken from me.

Yet, to be fair, I am aware that the earth needs this water. The excellent beach weather, which has drawn throngs to the water's edge, has not been good for the drying land. The continuously glorious sunshine has not permitted water to fall on the parched crops. The grasses have been turning brown. Reservoir levels are dipping dangerously low. The dusty earth has been longing for a good wash.

I think of that time long ago when the prophet Elijah stood against 450 prophets of Baal calling a nation to repentance. "If God is the Lord, follow him," he said to the people and proceeded to prepare the setting for God to graphically demonstrate his power. When God did show his greatness and the people worshiped him, we read, "The heavens grew black with clouds and wind, and there was a great rain . . .And the hand of the Lord was on Elijah." The rain was a sign of God's pleasure.

Could this be so today? I must, then, set aside my petulance and think of the earth which has longed for compassionate clouds.

71

There is a further lesson here, I know. There have been times of dryness in my spiritual life when I have forgotten to set aside times to pray. I tend to work at high speed with seemingly inexhaustible energy. My mind works on even when I wish to be at rest. In this activist mood, it is easy to forget that my energy will eventually run out if it is not replenished. Good works are fine as long as they are motivated from a center with a compass pointing toward God. I, too, need rain; a bath in God's spirit will fill the roots and crannies of my spiritual life.

I gaze reflectively through the glass wall of my living room and am astonished to see previously wilted geranium petals now lift full-orbed blossoms skyward. The grass is turning green before my eyes. The earth is literally beaming. I can echo the words of the poet Joyce Rupp as she watched a driving rain:

> The earth is coming alive this morning:
> Its hard dried land is given another chance.
> Baptized anew with showers of energy
> urged once more to fullness of growth.
>
> As I gaze upon these earth-born raindrops
> I am happied in their rinsing, washing touch
> Sensing the freshness that is in their song
> Hope filled to know so much life is close at hand.
>
> And in my own life, Lord: dried land,
> And in my own spirit, Lord: dusty soil,
> And in my own heart, Lord: hardened earth.
>
> I beg for raindrops of grace in my own life.
> The country of my heart needs a God-washing
> to rinse off the windows of unloving
> to bless the fragments of a tired heart.

I will enjoy the beach again tomorrow, and I am no longer sad that I will not be there today.

Our heavenly Father, author of every good and perfect gift, we thank you for the rain that revives our world. We thank you also for thy Spirit, which replenishes our soul. Help us ever to lift our weary soul to thee; in Jesus' name. Amen.

When Should We Accommodate?

Thou dost show me the path of life.
—Psalm 16:11*a*

Four-eyed fish? My own two eyes rest on *The National Geographic's* picture of the *Anableps* of the Amazon River who have built-in bifocals. I am relaxing in my sand chair at the beach and catching up on my neglected winter reading. I stare in amazement at the *Anableps'* eye where speckled tissue divides it at the waterline creating two pupils. One pupil is for seeing above the water, and the other for looking at underwater objects. Traveling in swarms as they do they form an odd goggle-eyed patrol.

Nature designed this special equipment so the four-eyed fish could lunge into the air for flying insects or dip under the water's surface to snap up unwary smaller swimmers. Nutrient-rich mud is a favorite haunt because the fish can hide in it and because it provides some food. Adept in both mud and water, the *Anableps* have adapted to the life they must lead.

From the Amazon my thoughts wander to the North, while my magazine falls in my lap. I can read only so long in the warm sun before I relax, drowsily lulled by the hypnotic sound of the waves. I muse lazily that nature has assisted in accommodating in our area too. I think of the wild roses growing in pink profusion among the beach grass. That cluster on the banking behind me is like a bouquet arranged by a giant. The sea air seems to make these roses more beautiful than their ancestors that arrived on our shores from Asia. "No Italian or artificial rose-garden could equal them," Thoreau once wrote. Growing on our beaches, seemingly nourished only by sand and salt air, the salt-spray rose thrives. Its blossoms perfume the air.

I wonder about accommodation. How does this apply to humans? We move to a new home, and we learn to accommodate—to enjoy it; or we are forever unhappy, looking backward to the past. We try a new job, and unless we accommodate we will not be happy or successful at our work.

Yet are there occasions when we accommodate too much? If we accommodate our ideals and our principles, are we doing what God wants?

The four-eyed fish and the wild Cape roses have no choice. They must accommodate or die. But we are called to a different and higher life-style. We have been given charge of the natural world. "Have dominion over the fish of the sea and over the birds of the air and over every living thing that moves upon the earth. . . . Behold I have given you every plant yielding seed which is upon the face of all the earth and every tree with seed in its fruit."

We are different, then. We must exercise our knowledge. We must make wise decisions. We must make moral judgments if we are to be fit custodians of the earth and all its creatures.

Accommodation then is not clear-cut for us as it is for the lesser creatures. We must stay close to our Creator to be sure that our decisions and our actions are in his will for the world. There will be times when we should accommodate and other times when we should firmly say no.

It is not as easy to be a human as it is to be an *Anableps* or a salt-spray rose. But it is much more challenging and rewarding. Also, if we echo the cry of David the psalmist, "Thou dost show me the path of life," and put our trust in God, we can know the secret of when to accommodate and when to refuse to go along with actions and choices that are not in his will.

Our loving heavenly Father, who carest about each one of your creations, whether inanimate or animate, help us to remain on the true pathway of life. Guide us so that we will have sufficient knowledge to follow the path and give us strength to remain on that path whatever the cost; in Jesus' name. Amen.

Out of Seeming Desolation

I know that thou canst do all things, and that no purpose of thine can be thwarted.
—Job 42:2

Once in a great while I forsake my lovely beach on the southern shore of Cape Cod and drive across the peninsula to its northern edge. In Cape Cod Bay there is no gulf stream to warm the water, and the tide varies much more than on the southern shores. When the moon is full, the tide on the northern shore can vary as much as twelve feet. The corresponding low tide reveals a new world of mud flats that is never seen the rest of the month.

At first these mud flats seem forsaken and desolate, anything but interesting places to wade and walk. But as I sink into the soft black ooze, I see a new and vibrant world. Claire Leighton, author of the book *Where Land Meets Sky,* appreciates mud flats. She writes they are "a whole earth in microcosm with Lilliputian valleys and hills, gorges and plateaus . . . a tiny river flows swiftly around the cliffs of sand. Against this diminutive setting it might be a Ganges or a Mississippi."

The flats are anything but inanimate and desolate. As I wait quietly, feeling like Gulliver in the land of Lilliput, I sense motion all around me. The water swirls and recedes. The mud pulsates and vibrates. Faint sucking sounds come from scallops buried underneath the ooze. The only things unmoving are discarded clam and oyster shells half buried in the mud, but even a few of these have living snails attached. A scratching sound causes me to turn. Two tiny crabs are fearfully scurrying away from my giant shadow. Small silver fish caught in a tide pool swim in circles waiting to be released when the tide turns. Farming the sea makes more sense to me now as I think of the endless cycle of life continuing ceaselessly independent of mankind.

Suddenly I feel a new pulse in the water around me, and I realize the tide has turned. I turn too and hasten toward the shore, knowing the incoming water will be swift and high. A last look at the flats as I reach the beach shows them desolate and forsaken again. But I know better. It is only an illusion, for they are actually filled with life and promise.

As I drive homeward I think of how these mud flats are like some human lives. They look unpromising and unlovely. Yet they have promise and growth possibilities if we look closely.

One of the most striking examples of this is the story of one of the thalidomide babies. You will recall that some European mothers-to-be who had this drug prescribed for them in the 1960s bore hideously deformed babies. One, named Eric, was born without legs and with only flippers for arms. At first he was institutionalized because of his handicaps even though he had a brilliant brain. Fortunately a loving couple was attracted to him and after many hospital calls took him home regularly to visit. Finally they adopted him. The father, a born inventor, spent all his spare time and whatever money he had constructing a vehicle that would make his young son mobile and independent. The final design, the fourth little car made, not only gave Eric complete independence but also is now benefiting other handicapped people around the world.

Forsaken and desolate? Unpromising and unlovely? Nothing is, with keen observation, love, determination, and the help of God.

Our loving Father who made all life, whether promising or unpromising, give us keen eyes to see the possibilities inherent in all things. Help us to work toward the development of all so that what seems unlovely will be beautiful and what seems desolate will be aglow; in Jesus' name. Amen.

The Challenge of Salt

You are the salt of the earth.
            —Matthew 5:13*a*

One cannot be by the sea for very long without being conscious of salt. A salty tang permeates the atmosphere, especially on damp and foggy days. A frolic in the water invariably brings at least one mouthful of water which causes a grimace because it is so salty. Now we think of salt as being an integral part of this place we love, but once it was more than that. This salt from the sea was economically important some one hundred or so years ago. Before the days of freezers, salt was essential as a preservative. It was especially important to fishermen who fished long distances at sea and needed to preserve their catch for home markets.

When imported salt became very expensive because of high taxes in the 1700s, the canny Cape Codders thought of the salt in the surrounding waters with more than casual interest. First attempts at extracting the salt from the sea were primitive. Water was carried in pails to vats, then left to evaporate or be boiled. This laborious process required 400 gallons of water to secure one bushel of salt. Then Captain John Sears of Dennis, dismayed by the lack of salt due to the British blockade during the Revolution and challenged by the bounty offered for locally extracted salt, invented a faster method. Using a windmill he pumped seawater into a series of wide vats which allowed for much faster evaporation. Other folk further refined the process by inventing roofs on pivots that could be swung over the vats during rainstorms and lifted aside during sunny weather. By 1830 there were 442 individual saltworks ringing the Cape shore producing 500,000 bushels of salt yearly. All this because large amounts of salt were demanded as a preservative by a growing nation.

Salt has been important as a preservative throughout recorded history, and the time of Jesus was no exception. I like to think Jesus had this aspect of salt in mind when he called his followers the salt of the earth.

According to Webster's dictionary, a preservative keeps something from injury or harm and keeps items from spoiling. A Christian, then, has a two-fold task. He or she must keep the faith safe from injury or harm, as well as keep it from decaying. Both of these are monumental tasks.

I think of some later disciples who were true to this challenge to be the salt of the earth. John and Charles Wesley of England of the eighteenth century are good examples. They sought to revitalize from within the faith of the church in their day. Catching again the first-century commitment which was Jesus' call, they established "classes" for Bible study and prayer. These soon spread across the land. The resulting religious renewal that eventually culminated in Methodism brought a rebirth of morality in England. In fact, historians credit this revitalization of the faith with saving the country from a bloody revolution such as took place across the channel in France. The Wesley brothers were like salt, saving the faith and keeping their country from spoiling.

We too must be like salt if we follow the command of Jesus, preserving our faith and culture in our day. A very tall order, I think. But perhaps this monumental challenge is not so impossible when we consider that God's support and his presence are available in unlimited supply.

Our ever-present heavenly Father, who hast promised strength for every task, give us the power to be preservers of the faith in whatever area we touch. Give us courage to tackle the tasks before us, as well as knowledge of your constant enabling presence; in Jesus' name. Amen.

A Pinch of Salt

*If salt has lost its taste, how shall its
saltness be restored? It is no longer
good for anything except to be thrown
out and trodden under foot by men.*
—Matthew 5:13b-14

The fog was extra thick this morning. As I walked down the road for the morning paper, the salty tang was so pronounced I could almost taste it. I was immediately reminded that salt is not only a preservative; it is also a flavoring. Cooks almost invariably add a pinch of salt when cooking to bring out the flavor. This action continues in spite of warnings that too much salt is bad for the health. A *tiny* bit of salt seems quite essential.

Common salt, or sodium chloride, is a compound widely distributed in nature. In addition to being in seawater, salt is also found in solid form such as rock salt or in liquid brine springs. Deposits of salt are found in many places in the world and probably are the residue from ancient seas. Salt has been essential for man and animals since time began. Great blocks of salt containing other nutrients as well are placed in pastures for cattle. Packages of salt containing iodide, another necessary nutrient for humans, are found on all grocery shelves. Natural-food addicts particularly favor salt recovered from the sea over that found in mines.

Apparently Jesus was well aware that a pinch of salt works wonders for any dish and makes a dramatic difference in the taste. In the Sermon on the Mount he made it abundantly clear that those who followed him were to flavor the place in which they lived, and if their saltiness were lost they would be worthless. Since only a tiny amount was needed to improve flavor, I believe he was also saying that it doesn't take many committed souls to make a great difference in a town, village,

80

or nation. This is surely a relief and encouragement to Christians who try to influence their surroundings but are often discouraged by seemingly overwhelming odds.

It is close to noon now, and the sun is shining strongly. The fog is gone, leaving only a rapidly dissipating mist on the water. But I muse on about the flavor of salt and how Christians in the past who were minuscule in number made a great impact in their era. Hawaii and a handful of missionaries come to mind. This paradise of the Pacific, known earlier as the Sandwich Islands, was inhabited by natives. In the eighteenth century, whites "discovered" the islands while on long whaling and trading voyages. The influence of these early whites was not the best since their purpose was commercial. The islands were a blend of easygoing ways and avarice. Then in 1820, seven men and their wives and children arrived who were different. They came to transplant a life they had found to be good, literally obeying Christ's command to "go ye into all the world and preach the gospel." These seven families were joined by others who assisted in putting the Hawaiian language in writing and printed the "talking leaves," or books. Bibles, primers, school books, and notices flowed from the printing presses. Soon schools, clinics, and churches "raised up a whole people . . . a nation to be enlightened and renovated and added to the civilized world."

There were not many workers to accomplish the monumental task; yet but a century later the descendants of these first native Hawaiian Christians have taken their place as leaders in government, the professions, and the arts. When the island centennial was celebrated, leaders from the mainland joined prominent Hawaiians in festive ceremonies. Churches of all faiths are still a dominant force on all the islands.

God of all ages, we thank you for the example of a handful of committed souls who made a great difference because they had not lost their flavor. Help us to resolve to make a difference where we live, that the moral decay eating at the heart of our civilization may be stopped and a healthy new life developed; in Jesus' name. Amen.

The Derelict

Therefore put away all filthiness and rank growth of wickedness and receive with meekness the implanted word, which is able to save your souls.
—James 1:21

A derelict has arrived in Hall Creek. Lodged in a crevice in the mud bank, the dory lies half submerged in the water, her wooden sides cracked and her gray paint flaking. There is no name or number on her. Forlorn and alone she rests, seemingly too aged to perform any work on the water again.

I am reminded of a verse from David McCord's poem "The Old Bateau":

Who has not seen the old bateau
Drift lonely to the lake below
Her river-driving days
Forgotten as the ways
Of sapling spruce that launched her long ago
The year of April snow?

Can this old bateau be reclaimed? I wondered. Then I remembered how some fifteen years ago our two sons and a friend found just such a derelict dory in this same creek. With youthful enthusiasm they pulled it onto dry land, replaced the broken pieces, outfitted her with new oarlocks, bought a motor, and gave her a new coat of paint. The reconditioned *Lapelou* (for the first letters of *Larry, Pete,* and *Louis*) gave many more years of service out of Hall Creek and in Nantucket Sound.

There are others who have reclaimed ships. I recall reading in *Adventures, Blizzards and Coastal Calamities* by Edward Rowe Snow of an ingenious Yankee who astounded his compatriots with a salvaging miracle. The steamer *Sankaty* had caught fire while tied up in New Bedford, Massachusetts. A flaming menace to shipping and especially the old whaling ship *Morgan,* she drifted in the harbor. Gradually the *Sankaty* sank to the bottom, with only the stack and whistles remaining in sight.

Captain John Snow of Rockland, Maine, looked over the situation and was convinced the vessel would still run even though by this time she had been underwater for two months. Buying the *Sankaty* from the insurance company for the price of junk, he repaired the hole and pumped out the water. Jury rigging the burned wheel, he was able to float the vessel again. Clearing away the barnacles and "rank growth" that had developed in the wheelhouse, he guided it out of the harbor under its own power, even though legally it had to be tied to a tug, to the astonishment of New Bedfordites. The miracle was well publicized in Boston papers; so all Rockland was waiting. When the *Sankaty* steamed into the harbor, every craft on the water and every whistle on shore blew tribute to a favorite son. After that the *Sankaty* served as a ferry on Long Island Sound and as a minesweeper during the war. As far as we know, this salvaged craft is still steaming complacently somewhere.

I wonder about lives as well as old boats. Can lives be reclaimed too, even though some seem so far gone it would take a miracle? Of course they can be. James seems to reinforce this in our scripture of the day. There have been countless examples of transformation in the lives of individuals, from St. Augustine and St. Francis to modern-day folk like Chuck Colson and Eldridge Cleaver. Alcoholics Anonymous is full of such success stories, and the Dave Wilkerson's drug centers relate many more tales of young people having their lives being transformed into witnessing, productive Christian ones.

It isn't only from lives of sin and sadness that men have been transformed. I am thinking of Max Cleland, head of the Veterans' Administration in Washington, D.C., who in 1968 lost both legs and an arm in Vietnam. After a grenade explosion changed his life, he spent eighteen months in rehabilitation, then entered politics. He was the youngest member of the Georgia Senate, serving from 1970 to 1974. In 1975 he joined the U.S. Senate Veterans' Affairs Committee and in 1977 was appointed head of the Veterans' Administration. He readily credits faith and prayer with his success. He is a living witness that the power of God can transform seemingly derelict lives into powerhouses of love and service.

Loving God, who never gives up on seemingly useless people, we thank thee for thy inexhaustible supply of power. May we do all we can to assist others in the task of transformation; in Jesus' name. Amen.

Dark Thoughts

Fear thou not; for I am with thee: be
not dismayed; for I am thy God.
                        —Isaiah 41:10a KJV

We have been reading much of late about sharks. The movie *Jaws* was such a success that *Jaws II* was created. Now I hear it rumored that there will soon be another to make a trilogy.

I am reminded of John Ciardi's poem "The Shark":

My dear, let me tell you about the shark.
Though his eyes are bright, his thought is dark . . .

That one dark thought he can never complete
Of something—anything—somehow to eat.
Be careful where you swim, my sweet.

Sitting here at the edge of a serene sea with fluffy white clouds sailing calmly through an azure sky, it is hard to imagine such dark denizens of the deep. But we do know they exist and that some are man-eaters.

What has not been made clear is that they are not always prone to attack humans. Gerald Wellington tells of an experience he had with sharks off the Galapagos Islands, that strange volcanic archipelago that straddles the equator off Ecuador. Dropping into the blue water, Wellington and two companions descended into a large coral colony and were instantly surrounded by five solid-gray sharks. One passed inches beyond Wellington's face mask. Stepping into coral "foxholes," the divers watched as more sharks arrived to examine these two-legged creatures. Suddenly these sharks and all small fish disappeared abruptly. Looking upward the divers saw twenty-four massive hammerhead sharks arriving, drawn by the confusion.

85

"Hammerheads have been known to attack man, and we shared uncomfortable visions of being the entree on a shark feeding frenzy," recounts Wellington. "Yet at the same time we were captivated by their gracefulness." The humans remained quiet, and the queer creatures with eyes mounted on strange protuberances watched curiously. When their curiosity was finally satisfied, they swam away, to the divers' great relief.

I sometimes wonder if these creatures with dark thoughts are rather like the dark fears that swim around in our unconscious mind. Sometimes these are formless, but other times they are very real and threatening. We have all experienced how much more frightening these are at night when we awaken worried and troubled. How often these same fears lose some of their terror when daylight arrives.

We should never negate these fears and attempt to push them back into our subconscious, I believe. No matter how bad the experience, it is better to face it, examining all the aspects and implications. Known fears are somehow easier to handle than dark, unknown ones.

Also, calmness and confidence in the promises of God can allay these fears when we examine them in his light. "Fear not, I am with thee," is not an empty phrase.

E. Stanley Jones, noted missionary evangelist to India, tells of an incident in the Sat Tal Ashram, India, when one of the members opened a bookcase and discovered a hive of bees. Fearfully slamming the door, she fled. Startled bees pursued and stung her. Another member quietly approached the bookcase and removed the books one by one even though bees were crawling all over them. Since he was calm and deliberate, he was not stung at all. Dr. Jones commented that in the first instance "fear produced the thing feared." In the second, quiet and confidence enabled the Ashramite to overcome the problem.

God of all creatures, help us to understand and overcome our fears whether caused by something within or without. Give us confidence and strength to remain calm in the face of all difficulties; in Jesus' name. Amen.

The Backbone of a Jellyfish

Finally, be strong in the Lord and in the strength of his might.
    —Ephesians 6:10

I will never forget my first sighting of a jellyfish. Walking along the shore one morning early, I espied an odd-looking mound of amber and went closer to investigate. Lying half in and half out of the water, it undulated with the action of the waves. Long, wispy tentacles floated lazily on the water.

I was reminded immediately of times in my childhood when my mother would say, exasperated by my indecision, "You have the backbone of a jellyfish." So that's what she meant, I thought, examining the round, scallop-edged body that had obviously no backbone at all.

Later I came across an amusing poem by Sandra Hochman who had been as captivated by the jellyfish as I.

Love Song for a Jellyfish
How amazed I was, when I was a child,
To see your life on the sand.
To see you living in your jelly shape,
Round and slippery and dangerous.
You seemed to have fallen

Not from the rim of the sea,
But from the galaxies.
Stranger, you delighted me,
Weird object of the stinging world.

Now, once in a great while, jellyfish invade our beach, and I think again about backbones. How necessary they are for humans, if not for jellyfish! Fortunately we need not rely on ourselves alone to keep a firm backbone. Paul told the Ephesians to "be strong in the Lord and in the strength of his might." So we do have someone to lean on, to provide the power. We mustn't forget, though, that the commitment to make our backbone strong is still our job.

One of the favorite Christian books of all times is *In His Steps* by Charles Sheldon. In it a desperate, out-of-work tramp challenges a complacent congregation to act as Jesus did. Pastor Henry Maxwell and his upper-middle-class suburban parish, jolted by the young man's comments, determine to act as they felt Jesus would have acted throughout the next full year. The changes that resulted in the city and in the nation because of this commitment were amazing and thought-provoking. Plenty of backbone was needed and they had it, as, helped by their growing consciousness of the Holy Spirit, they were true to their resolve.

It would be interesting to see what a Christian novelist could make of a similar plot laid in the present day. Better still, it would be interesting to see what would result if each Christian determined to walk in Jesus' steps and kept a strong backbone with the help of God.

Thank you, jellyfish, for your reminder.

God of the spineless creatures as well as of those with backbones, help us to realize the importance of keeping our

*spiritual backbone strong and sturdy. Give us the courage and
the commitment to follow in Jesus' path throughout our days;
in Jesus' name. Amen.*

Toward a Limitless Horizon

> *Who will go over the sea for us, and*
> *bring it to us?*
> —Deuteronomy 30:13*b*

Along with rhododendrons and roses, the boats to
Nantucket and Martha's Vineyard operating out of Hyannis
are sure signs of spring. From our glass-walled living room we
can see the sleek white steamers plowing steadily through the
waves. We watch them often as they disappear over the
horizon, carrying people, goods, and sometimes cars and
trucks to the busy little island communities off the coast of
Massachusetts.

Often I think about this horizon, which actually is
something that does not exist. Webster's dictionary defines
horizon as "the apparent junction of earth and sky," or the
"range of perception or experience." A horizon, then, is
something that only seems to be, and it always exists in
relation to our own observation. Therefore, as we move it
moves. As we go forward our horizon extends.

Hans Sidon, a German-born minister of the gospel, writes
in his recent book *I Chose America* that he had long been
concerned about the problem of keeping a vision of worldwide
missions before his congregations. He had little difficulty in

enlisting the talents of his people in the solving of local needs but found it much harder to lift their hearts and minds to faraway needs.

Then one day he was watching a freighter leaving the harbor in Portsmouth, New Hampshire. "The freighter gradually disappeared. It had gone beyond the horizon—my own horizon." He suddenly realized that the horizon "is nothing but an indication of our limited vision. The higher man rises from the earth, the more the horizon recedes. . . . We can apply this to our Christian life. The higher we rise, the greater and farther will be our vision. The purpose of all Christian work is to make us see beyond the horizon."

Mission is an intriguing word. Jesus was engaged in mission, which began where he lived and extended beyond his horizon. At the time of his ascension he said to the disciples, "You shall be my witnesses in Jerusalem and in all Judea and Samaria and to the end of the earth." I like to think that, as he was caught up into heaven following these words, his rising and the consequent extension of the horizon were symbolic for his followers. If we truly follow him in any age, must not our horizon extend throughout our world?

Therefore, our mission is not only to those close by whose needs we can see but also to those across the wide seas in faraway lands whose needs are made known to us by missionaries, government leaders, newspapers, television, radio, magazines, and books.

True Christians are those who have learned to look well beyond their own physical horizon. When they are made aware of physical, moral, or spiritual needs they are disturbed. They cannot rest until some action is taken to alleviate that need. They are haunted by the cry coming from beyond their limited horizon. "Who will go over the sea for us and bring it to us?"

Our heavenly Father, who has no horizon, help us to feel the need of our brothers and sisters in faraway places as well as at home. Give us the will to keep our horizon unlimited and to answer human need as Christ commanded in the long ago; in Jesus' name. Amen.

Intimations of Eternity

> *Let not your hearts be troubled; believe in God, believe also in me. In my Father's house are many rooms; if it were not so, would I have told you that I go to prepare a place for you?*
> —John 14:1-2

There is something compelling about the seashore when it is absolutely devoid of other humans. This usually happens only in the early morning or late in the day at my beach. Ordinarily the wide sands and adjacent waters are filled with happy bathers, serious sun-tanners, children playing, teen-agers sailing, and others walking to and fro. Early in the day or when evening falls, when only the footprints of these happy ones dot the sand, the seashore has a different quality.

Ellen P. Von den Deale captured this mood completely in her poem "My Path," from which I quote a part.

> There is a path I walk
> From sand to sea,
> Reality of home to vast infinity.
> Before me is the quiet bay

An inlet from the sea.
Here the hand of God
Joins wind-swept white of clouds
To flaming lanterns
Hung in evening sky.
From water's edge I find my God
Where no man mars this sanctuary
Of the sea.

Even in the midst of winter I can shut my eyes and recall the aura of this quiet beach. It always evokes a meditative mood. It is at times like these that we feel the whisperings of eternity, the call of an unseen world beyond our own. We know with certainty that there is more to our surroundings than we can see with our eyes, feel with our hands, or hear with our ears.

In our day, thoughts of death and of a world beyond the grave are not often brought into conversations. Since hospitals have become the place to die, people do not as often see death occur. Children are not familiar with its naturalness, except as they see a beloved pet die. Yet death is part of the cycle of life and only a transition into another form of living. We should not hide thoughts of death but rather face them and deal with them honestly.

John Myers, author of the recent paperback *Voices from the Edge of Eternity,* felt called to write this book when he stumbled across an account of deathbed testimonies published in 1898. Here a cross section of people, young and old and from all walks of life, told of seeing quite clearly beyond the grave. "What they saw and sensed not only bears evidence as to the *fact* of man's immortality, but also answers many very pertinent questions that perplex the minds of thinking people today. . . . Far more important," he says, is the "glorious sense of goal and destiny which alone can defy the death grip of materialism which threatens to plunge our generation into the madness of purposeless life."

Other recent books on this same subject by Raymond Moody bring clear evidence that after this earthly life is over the soul will survive in a new and more wonderful state.

Somehow at the beginning or close of day on a quiet beach that reaches into infinity it is easier to feel the gentle stirrings of the world beyond. It is a comforting rather than a frightening sensation.

God of this world and the next, help us to feel the pulse of the world that is to come while we are still involved in this one. Instruct us in the ways that lead us to a certainty that when we leave this life we are actually going home to you; in Jesus' name. Amen.

The Shining Sea

And before the throne there is as it were a sea of glass, like crystal.
—Revelation 4:6

Today the sun is at such an angle to the water that there is a shining pathway across the sea. It is as if a thousand spotlights are glowing at once. Sunglasses are a necessity, and even with them I can't look straight at this gleaming trail.

I recall other times when the ocean is momentarily blinding. In winter during prolonged zero weather the bays and inlets freeze, and the ice floes create a magnificent mirror reflecting the sun. It is an eerie sight to see the gleaming flashes as the ice fields shift with wind and tide. There is also an eerie, grinding sound heard alongshore as the tide forces ice against ice, making it rise and fall in the intense cold.

Perhaps these two experiences are what Katharine Lee Bates, noted educator and poet, had in mind when she wrote the lines "God shed his grace on thee, / And crown thy good with brotherhood / From sea to shining sea" in "America the Beautiful." This scene was surely from her childhood home in Falmouth, Massachusetts, where she must often have seen the sea shining and reflecting both in winter and in summer sun.

I wonder if these shining-sea incidents are not indicative of occasional shining experiences in our life. Usually life is routine as we go through our days in the path we have chosen. Our work, our recreation, our friendships, our commitments to church, follow prosaic patterns. Then comes a shining moment when the routine falls away and we are caught up in a deeper experience.

I recall just such a moment several years ago when I was sitting in a Quaker meeting. I had come into the quiet room leaving the friendly greetings and laughter in the vestibule. Gradually as others arrived and settled down the silence became almost palpable. As I recall, the silence was broken only once by a sweet, white-haired woman who felt led to recite a verse of scripture. About thirty minutes into the silent worship, I began to sense a Presence close by yet just beyond. It is very difficult to explain. It seemed as if this Presence were a real personality; yet there was nothing visible to the eyes that could be described. The Presence was just beyond a thicket. It was up to me, I understood, to pull away the branches and thus "see" the Presence more clearly. Gradually this impression receded, but the remembrance of it is with me always. It is a great source of comfort. Could it be this same Presence that caused the psalmist to cry, "Even though I walk through the valley of the shadow of death, I fear no evil; for thou art with me"?

This was a shining moment in my life and one which comes

to mind whenever I see "seas of glass shining like crystal" on the gleaming summer water or on blinding winter ice.

God of all our days, we thank you for your unceasing presence through every second of every life. Thank you also for the shining moments that though eventually receding confirm thy constant presence; in Jesus' name. Amen.

Sea and Winged Creatures

And four great beasts came up out of
the sea, different from one another.
—Daniel 7:3

Most of us landlubbers are familiar with creatures at the edge of the sea. On a walk along our shores I often see the ancient horseshoe crab, an actual living fossil. A member of the spider family, its ancestors date back 400 million years. We of the temperate zones have many sea and winged creatures to enthrall us. But watchers in the tropics or on frigid Arctic shores have many creatures to view also. I recall being fascinated by pelicans on a visit to Key West in Florida. These awkward birds with their enormous beaks waited patiently on dockside pilings in anticipation of dinner from incoming fishing boats. In northern climes watchers can see ponderous, bewhiskered walruses as well as engaging, slippery seals. In the distance in all these climes can be seen spouting whales on their migrations. All of these are amazingly diverse creatures of the sea, any of which might be one of the four beasts the prophet Daniel mentioned.

One puzzle to me is how these winged creatures survive. Some, like gulls and sea ducks, can rest on the ocean surface, storing up energy for further flights. Their feathers contain an ointment that protects them from the wet and cold. But there are other winged creatures that fly over vast stretches of the ocean with seemingly no place to break their journey. Take the Monarch butterfly for example. This frail-looking creature rallies by the thousands in the early fall off Newfoundland and on islands like Martha's Vineyard for a trip south to a 9,500-foot volcanic mountain in Mexico. In this astonishing annual pilgrimage they fly at a 15-foot altitude going around city buildings, in and over coastal waters. They stop briefly to feed on flowers when available and cluster at night in trees when they are over land. I often wondered what they did at sea until I read that Monarch butterflies rest on the mast of fishing boats off Georges Bank.

I was further relieved to read in *The National Geographic* that tall ships are often a haven for birds in flight. Kenneth Garrett, who sailed with the beautiful *Dar Pomorza* from Poland to America during the Bicentennial rendezvous of tall ships, wrote that a pair of doves came aboard briefly. Later a tiny wren "alighted on his ankle and scurried up his trouser leg. Warmed and rested after a 45-minute visit, the wren emerged and took off for shore."

What preparation God has made for his creatures great and small. If he has plotted their pathways of migration and designed their food cycles, then surely he has as much concern for the two-legged folks he also brought into existence. Christ told us of God's concern for humans. "Fear not," he said, "you are of more value than many sparrows."

I find comfort in knowing that small birds take refuge with humans on the long sea journeys and that the intuitive travels of Monarch butterflies to Mexico and whales from southern to northern waters are so carefully planned by the Creator.

Perhaps we worry too much about our own survival and our

own special pathway. I know it is right to be concerned over something that should be changed, and we must take any action we can to cause the necessary change. But perhaps we are overly concerned, indeed anxious sometimes, when we should have more faith and trust.

"Look at the birds of the air," said Jesus, "they neither sow nor reap nor gather into barns, and yet your heavenly Father feeds them. Are you not of more value than they?"

When I become worried and distraught, I try to remember the great beasts of the sea and the winged fowl of the air for whom our Father cares. I think about the four-hundred-million-year-old crab at my feet. Then I become more content, turning to God in faith for help and strength.

God of all creatures, small and large, old and young, sea and winged, thank you for your caring and concern for all of these. Thank you also for your care for us. Give us the faith to rest on thy strength always as well as the will to work for change when it is necessary; in Jesus' name. Amen.

The Wind and the Spirit

*The wind blows where it wills; and
you hear the sound of it, but you do
not know whence it comes or whither
it goes; so it is with every one who is
born of the Spirit.*
—John 3:8

No one can live by the sea for very long and not be conscious
of the wind. Sometimes it is a gentle breeze that teases the
book one is reading and pushes beach balls along the sand.
Other times it is so threatening that blankets and towels are
hastily gathered, and a quick retreat is made from the shore.
In summer the breezes are bearable, except perhaps during a
rain-driven northeaster. In winter the winds bite into the very
marrow of one's bones, and the inclination is to remain inside
by a glowing hearth.

The effects of the wind are particularly noticeable along the
edge of the sea. When the winds of a northeaster whip the
waters into a white frenzy and howl around the edges of the
old captains' houses, they also beat against the shore with
equal fury. They play tricks with the sand dunes, sometimes
changing their shapes not only from one weird form into
another equally eerie one, but also into an entirely new
location. After one particularly fierce storm, a huge dune that
stood overlooking Nauset Beach slid into the sea as if
surrendering to the insistent, forceful buffeting of the wind.
Along one stretch of dunes the wind had carved grotesque
figures reminiscent of the Grand Canyon. The roots of the
usually firm beach grass were exposed, and in the sand
tracings around them one could see effects of the wild dance
the wind had forced upon the helpless grasses.

At times like these we are reminded of Jesus' words about
the Holy Spirit, the Comforter, who was given as the Divine

successor to the Christ. The Holy Spirit continues and further unfolds the work of Jesus in a unique way. He dwells within the heart of humans and gives guidance in all truth.

But how can we explain the Holy Spirit? The best description still seems to be the words of Jesus that liken the Spirit to the wind. We cannot see the wind, only its effects. We cannot predict its passage. It goes where it wills. We have no control over the wind. It blows vigorously or gently, depending on its own wishes.

So also is the Holy Spirit. He works in the hearts of humans, and where the individuals permit it, lives are transformed. The results are so obvious they are noted by others. The Holy Spirit comes and goes at his own speed, constantly at work in those who are open to him. We accept and respond but do not control the pace. Sometimes it is a gentle prompting that we feel. At other times it is a mighty sweep of emotion. But always, if we are responsive, changes come in our life and in the life of those around us.

Dr. E. Stanley Jones explains it clearly in his book *The Word Became Flesh.* "Up to this point in our study of the Word become flesh it has been on the outside—in history [Jesus]. . . . The commandments from this time on were from within—through the Holy Spirit." When Jesus finished his earthly task, he deliberately chose to exercise his authority from within. "He speaks from within and awaits our inner consent before it becomes manifest . . . for Divine Wisdom knows that only as we willingly and gladly consent to cooperate with the Word, will that Word become flesh in us."

It is then that the effects of the Spirit are seen, just as the effects of the wind are seen but never the wind itself.

Our Father God, author of all truth, help us to feel and recognize the promptings of thy Spirit. Give us strength and wisdom to follow these promptings so that we may develop into the persons you expect us to become; in Jesus' name. Amen.

On Migrations

Was it not thou that didst dry up the
  sea,
the waters of the great deep;
that didst make the depths of the sea a
  way
for the redeemed to pass over?
                    —Isaiah 51:10

It is intriguing to imagine as one gazes at a gently rolling seascape the many forms of life that are migrating within it. Every spring we try to make a pilgrimage to see one migration in process—that of the herring. There are several herring runs nearby where we can stand in awe of the instinct that drives these big-eyed silver fish upstream, hurtling over any obstacle in their way. These herring, or alewives, live in the ocean except for the time of spawning. Then they swim unerringly, not to just any freshwater stream but to the very place where they were spawned. Schools of these herring enter the marshes and press inland. They swim against the current, leaping upstream over fish ladders to reach their place of birth. It is a difficult task, but the herring persist and spawn a new generation. This ageless cycle has been continuing since before recorded history, and the annual spring appearances were heralded by Wampanoags and Pilgrims.

Another migration has been noted only in recent years. Eels have been long known along this coast, but the place of their birth in the Sargasso Sea has been a more recent discovery. Apparently these serpentlike fish originate in the salty waters off Bermuda and swim north with the gulf stream. They swim into tidal creeks along our coast. Tiny and transparent, they arrive by the tens of thousands. Gradually as they find homes in the fresh waters of streams, their skin darkens, and they grow quite long. These eels burrow in the mud during daylight hours and hunt for fish at night. Each fall great numbers of them wiggle through the marshy inlets and embark on their two-month trip to Bermuda waters. Here at great depths among the Sargasso weeds, they spawn and die.

My mind drifts back to Bible times and another migration. This time it is of humans, Israelites, who were called by God and led by Moses out of Egypt to the Promised Land. Their trip was hazardous. After the plagues of Egypt and a reluctant release by Pharaoh, they were pursued by his chariots. Faced with a hopeless situation, Pharaoh's armies behind and the Red Sea before, the Israelites lost faith and wept. It was then as the Scripture records that God "didst make the depths of the sea a way for the redeemed to pass over." Freely they passed to the other shore to begin forty years of wandering in the wilderness before they finally reached their destination, Canaan.

Slow though it was, I believe it was a genuine migration. So also did William Bradford, governor of the fledgling Pilgrim colony at Plymouth, Massachusetts. Writing in his history of Plymouth Plantation, he likens the wanderings of the Israelites to the migration of the Pilgrim colony from England, to Holland, and finally to the New World—the new Canaan. This analogy followed the Pilgrim story, for Peter Gay wrote later in *A Loss of Mastery: Puritan Historians in Colonial America,* "Like the children of Israel, the English had erred in the wilderness and come at last to a promised land."

But don't individuals migrate as well as do nature's creatures and nations? Aren't all of us in a sense in migration? Probably not, I muse, in the same fashion as the Pilgrims or the Israelites; yet aren't we individually migrating through this life toward a goal in the next one? As we grow, transform, proceed through the years, aren't we migrating toward another home? Though, as Paul says, "we see through a glass, darkly" right now, we are called in this life to develop to our full potential and to struggle in a personal migration toward a new and different life that we will one day see more clearly.

Our Father, who dost oversee the migration of all your creatures, whether of the natural world, of nations, or of individuals, help us to see more clearly our own personal migration. Give us the wisdom to discern the path as well as the courage to follow where it leads; in Jesus' name. Amen.

Undiscovered Country

> *For there is nothing hid, except to be made manifest; nor is anything secret, except to come to light.*
> —Mark 4:22 RSV

I am convinced most of us go through life unaware that there is an undiscovered country all around us. We have become so insulated in our tight little houses and our compact automobiles that our contact with the real out-of-doors is often minimal. Time was when we grew our food, milked our cows, cut our firewood, and had firsthand contact with nature. But now modern inventions and methods have insulated us so much from our environment that we sometimes rarely notice it. We are apt to fuss about the weather if it affects our plans, or we may notice an exceptional sunset as we leave the office for home, but seldom do we actually take time to understand the natural world in which we live. That is why natural history guides are so welcome. They give us the benefit of all that scholars have learned and enable us to walk through our days with eyes that see with new vision.

Such a book is *The Outer Lands,* an explanation of the natural world of Cape Cod, Martha's Vineyard, Nantucket, Block Island, and Long Island. Written by Dorothy Sterling, the all-encompassing volume immerses us in the undiscovered country around us. She describes it thus:

Waves and wind, sun and fog have shaped the sandy substance left behind by Ice Age glaciers to create a landscape strikingly different from that of the mainland, while the lands' proximity to the sea has given them a unique plant and animal life. There are broad beaches of white sand, shimmering dunes and green salt meadows. There are quiet ponds, rolling moors and twisted pines.

Eagerly I dip into the pages of this volume which promises to tell me so much about these places of sea wind and salt spray.

At the same time another part of my mind is wondering if there is a parallel here to the life of the Spirit. Have we not much undiscovered country within ourselves too? In the book *The Spirit of Synergy,* Robert Keck is apparently of the same mind. In an effort to free himself from continued, agonizing back pain, he investigated faith healing, psychic healing, acupuncture, biofeedback, and medical hypnosis. To his great surprise he found they had many similarities, and they were related also to meditative prayer. He comes to the conclusion that "we are using only a small percentage of our physical, mental and spiritual abilities." Then he asks: "No one in business will be successful using only 10 percent of his resources. Can we Christians be satisfied with burying 90 percent of the talents God has given us?"

Taking us on his own pilgrimage, Keck points out ways we can unlock the latent power within us by using four techniques of meditative prayer.

There seems to be a spate of books on this subject of developing our inner potential just now. It must be a felt need in our society. After reading this book, I made a mental note to take further excursions into the realm of the spirit as well as my natural world, hoping to become more familiar with the undiscovered country in both places.

I shall take heart in my quest from the words of Jesus: "For there is nothing hid except to be made manifest; nor is anything secret except to come to light." I believe we all were meant to embark on this quest.

Our Father God, ruler of the world we know as well as of undiscovered mysteries, grant us the will and the patience to enter the life of meditative prayer. Help us to quiet our minds and hearts so that the undiscovered country within us will be made manifest; in Jesus' name. Amen.

Learning from
the Horseshoe Crab

*Let the waters bring forth swarms of
living creatures.*
—Genesis 1:20*a*

On a walk along the sandy shore most any day, I see empty
shells of the horseshoe crab close to the tide line. At first I was
puzzled by the many brown shells, tough as armor plates,
littering the beach. The inside of each shell is plainly empty,
with no sign of its previous inhabitant; it seemed unlikely a
predator had seized upon the crab for food. Surely if that
were the case a few shreds of the unfortunate victim would
remain.

A little research revealed that these shells are castoffs, the
result of the crab's growth. These descendants of the giant
water scorpions of the Paleozoic era molt regularly as they
grow. The crabs are perpetuated when each spring the eggs
are laid by the female and fertilized by the male. Sand lightly
covers the eggs as they develop in the warm sun. High spring
tides carry tiny inch-long crabs into the flats where they
burrow into the sand. The crabs grow slowly, eventually
reaching maturity about the age of nine years, having grown
an additional eight inches or so. During these various growth
stages the crabs shed one shell and grow another. They
accomplish this by crawling headfirst through a slit in the front
using the five pairs of tiny legs. The empty shells are then cast
adrift and float toward the shore.

The horseshoe crab not only molts as it grows but also
adapts beautifully to its environment. During daylight hours it
"lays low" on the ocean bottom, using the front of its shell as a
plow and using its legs to propel itself through the sand. At
night, when ready to swim, it flips over on its back using the

shell as a skiff. The ten legs move in unison like a rowing crew, propelling the crab easily through the water.

Both attributes of growth and adaptation are intriguing. Could these be keys to the crab's survival for 400 million years?

Humans grow approximately in the same proportion and also mature in a series of stages. Sometimes, however, the body grows, but humans fail to cast off their personality shell. Occasionally we find a very immature individual remaining in an adolescent stage though inhabiting a mature body. The problems occasioned thereby don't need to be spelled out here. The results are all around us as marriages dissolve, mental cases mount, child abuse grows, and court dockets clog. Surely we must somehow find more help for individuals in the growing stages so their personalities "molt" as their bodies grow.

Adaptation is crucial too. It is important to have great dreams and to set high goals. But it is dangerous to ignore our surroundings and exist in a dream world. We must accept and face what and where we are before we can make realistic plans and goals for future development.

It is tempting to wonder if the horseshoe crab was one of the very first to swim the seas when God said, "Let the waters bring forth swarms of living creatures." I also wonder if this same ten-legged crab were meant to bring a message to the two-legged folks on land. When we see its cast-off shells littering the beach, perhaps we are meant to recall the importance of maturing and adapting.

Dear Father of all creatures, help us to learn from nature. Give us the impetus to study the world around us and deduce messages for mankind. Help us also to learn these lessons for ourselves, shedding immature ways and establishing realistic goals; in Jesus' name. Amen.

Build Thee
More Stately Mansions

But grow in the grace and knowledge
of our Lord and Savior Jesus Christ.
—II Peter 3:18

Rainy days are an excellent time to visit museums, especially if vacation days at the beach are numbered and one is thirsty for more knowledge about the sea. Here in these unique treasure houses are found many aspects of marine life and times. Though every museum near the shore has a variety of artifacts brought home by globe-girdling mariners of past centuries, there is invariably one artifact that is always present. It is the huge, chambered nautilus shell with its interior of lustrous pearly pink overflowing onto the grayish outer lip.

These remarkable mollusks of the ancient Cephalopoda family are found in the Pacific and Indian oceans as well as in other warm eastern seas. Their remarkable mother-of-pearl luster has earned them the name *pearly nautilus*. Since Cape Cod and other New England deep-sea captains were familiar with the Pacific Ocean and all the waters in between, it is no wonder that many fine examples of the pearly nautilus found their way here.

No doubt curious folks then as well as now carefully examined these shells noting their unusual construction. A young nautilus, it seems, lives in a bent shell. As the mollusk grows the shell increases in a spiral fashion, and the mollusk periodically draws itself outward, closing the door behind it. A chambered spiral results, which when cut open reveals a unique creation.

One of these nautilus observers of a century ago was Oliver

Wendell Holmes of Boston, who wrote the now classic poem "The Chambered Nautilus."

Its webs of living gauze no more unfurl;
  Wrecked is the ship of pearl!
  And every chambered cell,
Where its dim dreaming life was wont to dwell,
As the frail tenant shaped his growing shell,
  Before thee lies revealed,—
Its irised ceiling rent, its sunless crypt unsealed!

Year after year beheld the silent toil
  That spread his lustrous coil;
  Still, as the spiral grew,
He left the past year's dwelling for the new,
Stole with soft step its shining archway through,
  Built up its idle door,
Stretched in his last-found home, and knew the old no more.

Holmes was caught with the significance of the mollusk's action of shedding the old, smaller compartment for the new and larger room, as well as the significance when applied to humans. Today's authors are fascinated with this subject too. Witness the sweeping popularity of Gail Sheehy's book *Passages* which documents the various stages of life. Think also of the increasing emphasis on making a second career in the retirement years. Life is more and more considered to be a cycle of growth rather than a period of waiting for death after the major work of life is done. Surely this is what Peter meant by "growing in grace." We must seek to continually enlarge our personal environment so that our souls will be larger also.

Consequently, as we gaze at a pearly nautilus we can agree with Holmes' closing stanza:

Build thee more stately mansions, O my soul,
  As the swift seasons roll!
  Leave thy low-vaulted past!

Let each new temple, nobler than the last,
Shut thee from heaven with a dome more vast,
  Till thou at length are free,
Leaving thine outgrown shell by life's unresting sea!

*Our Father God, creator of the mollusk as well as of ourselves,
give us the vision to move confidently through life's stages,
always expanding our horizons and our souls; in Jesus' name.
Amen.*

Growing Pearls

*Again, the kingdom of heaven is like a
merchant in search of fine pearls,
who, on finding one pearl of great
value, went and sold all that he had
and bought it.*
          —Matthew 13:45

A Provincetown, Massachusetts, constable was dining on
steamed quahogs recently when he bit on something hard that
almost broke a tooth. Taking the quahog out of his mouth, he
found to his astonishment that it contained a pearl.

"I've eaten a lot of quahogs over the years, but this was my
favorite," he later noted, displaying the jewel with pride.
According to the newspaper account, the rare pearl is
cone-shaped with a flat bottom. Its deep purple color glows
with a white luster. Dr. Charles Mayo, a marine biologist, has
vouched for the pearl's authenticity.

Dropping the newspaper account I thought about pearls.

Though more often found in oysters than in quahogs, in both they result from a calamity. A rough bit of sand or a tiny rock fragment invades the oyster's (or quahog's) shell. This hurts, and the oyster tries very hard to push it out. It struggles to eject this foreign object, twisting and turning in every direction, all to no avail. The tiny invader remains. Finally the oyster gives up in despair, determining to live with the discomfort. Then two things happen. The pain seems easier to bear, and a crystal fluid begins to coat the rock fragment or piece of sand. Gradually a round, smooth-surface cover develops that grows larger and richer in color every day. While the oyster or quahog pays no more attention, within its heart the ugly intruder is growing into a beautiful pearl.

I meditated upon the lustrous pearl that results from an unlovely happening. Similar things sometimes happen in the life of humans. Sometimes an individual is quite ordinary and unremarkable, one who would not particularly stand out in a crowd as a leader or as an exceptionally fine character. Then adversity comes followed by a period of anguish over the hurt. The trouble could be physical or emotional; the hurt is just as real. The temptation is to succumb to self-pity, and many do.

Yet sometimes from ordinary individuals come unsuspected depths. A faith arises that enables the person to accept the trouble and ask God's help in bearing it. A beautiful grace then comes into that person's life and eventually the trial is changed to a blessing, and a jewel of character begins to develop.

I have a friend who is a jewel. Stricken with polio at the age of nine, she accepted her limitations and went on to make a beautiful life for herself. She authored six books, became an accomplished musician, and developed extensive knowledge of world literature. Though paralyzed from the waist down, she lives by herself in an especially built house. She hosts a Great Books group, is immersed in writing her autobiography, belongs to a writers' club, and until recently wrote the program notes for the Cape Cod Symphony concerts. No one who stops in to visit her is reminded of her physical state. Instead, the talk is of current events, news of mutual friends, and the next project in the typewriter.

I am delighted for our Provincetown constable's unexpected treasure, but I revel more in the many people like my friend who have triumphed over difficulties. Having grown in grace into living jewels, these are surely like the pearl of great value in the scripture, for they hold in their heart the kingdom of heaven.

Our gracious Father, when sorrows come, help us to face them with courage and faith. Give us grace that we may grow jewels of character that will be luminous spiritual beacons to others; in Jesus' name. Amen.

Steady as an Iceberg

Therefore take the whole armor of God, that you may be able to withstand in the evil day, and having done all, to stand.
—Ephesians 6:13

We don't see icebergs in the warmer waters, but part of the year these monstrous floating masses of ice that break off from Arctic glaciers are very real hazards in the sea. Though their size varies, it is not uncommon in the north Atlantic to see bergs 10 to 100 feet high, with towers and spires jutting upward 200 to 250 feet. One of the earliest icebergs mentioned in literature was cited in the medieval text *Voyage of Saint Brendan,* which tells of an Irish abbot-explorer and his monks who voyaged to the New World seeking "the land promised to the saints" about A.D. 600. On their hazardous journey toward what we know as Newfoundland, the adventurers sighted a "crystal column," which could only be an iceberg.

In May of 1976 Timothy Severin and four others sought to recreate the ancient voyage in conditions as nearly like the original as possible. Named *The Brendan,* their thirty-six-foot boat of leather and wood with Celtic crosses on the sails proved seaworthy even when it ran into present-day "crystal columns" in great number. "It was a sight to send the adrenaline racing—all around and ahead of us were jagged monsters of ice . . . a nightmare jumble of individual floes." That *The Brendan* survived the deadly passage between the icebergs with only one jagged tear in the leather, which was promptly mended, is a tribute to the seaworthiness of those long-ago vessels.

After reading about this tremendously interesting experience in the December, 1977, issue of *The National Geographic,* I began thinking about icebergs.

According to the encyclopedia, only one-seventh of the ice in an iceberg is seen. That leaves six-sevenths under water. The ice columns float down from the ice fields of Greenland, Hudson Bay, and the Spitzbergen Sea, threatening ships particularly in April, May, and June. They sail serenely southward seemingly unaffected by surface currents. Since their great mass reaches far down into the ocean, their movement is guided by the deep ocean currents; so they surge steadily ahead undeterred by surface buffeting.

Icebergs are a reminder of the strength and stability that can be ours too if we reach deep and draw on the immeasurable resources of God. If we open our heart to the transforming power of the Holy Spirit and let him work his way in our life, we develop a strength and a depth that cause us to stand firm in troubles, unmoved by surface squalls. Then when temptation comes or when the crowd calls us to follow a lower way, we can reach deep into our spiritual currents and find the power to stand firm in what we believe is the right path. In the words of Paul, we thus put on the whole armor of God that we "may be able to withstand in the evil day."

Whenever I see chunks of ice along the shore on winter days I think of the "crystal columns" to the north of us and how stable they are as they sail the ocean currents. I hope to sail in deep spiritual waters like the iceberg and be better able to withstand the temptations and trials of life.

Creator of the natural world, help us to see in your inanimate creations messages appropriate for ourselves. Like the massive icebergs, may six-sevenths of us extend deeply into your spiritual realm; in Jesus' name. Amen.

Dominion from Sea to Sea

May he have dominion from sea to sea,
and from the River to the ends of the earth!
—Psalm 72:8

A storm has subsided—a three-day fury of a northeaster—and I am well aware that the will of the Lord in his natural world prevails over the wishes of mankind. For generation after generation through prehistory as well as recorded history, mariners have known this too, that the hand of the Lord is everywhere and his complete dominion is from sea to sea. There is nothing like the fury of nature to put humans in their place!

In the last century a New England sea captain testified to this in his ship's log. On December 31, 1854, Captain Tristram Jordan was aboard the ship *Pepperell* which was leaving New Orleans for Liverpool, England. He wrote:

The last day of this year, light airs from the northwest, smooth sea, clear sky, and a beautiful sunset far from home. God only knows what the ensuing year may bring forth. . . . Oh! That I may be as calm, my hopes as clear, and my sunset as clear as the day that has passed. Faith in God."

Captain Jordan had been to sea thirty-three years, and according to his great grandson Alfred T. Hill writing in the book *Voyages,* he had "survived a shipwreck off Cape Cod, suffered illnesses, encountered mutiny and desertion, seen men fall from the rigging to their watery graves." He had witnessed enough disasters to "drive the fear of God deep into his soul."

As I walked by the calm sea that held only an excess of flotsam carried in by the waves to remind me of the fury of the previous days, I thought of the great whaling ships that had set out from these shores on voyages of three to five years. Surely they too felt the dominion of God from sea to sea.

Ishmael, the protagonist in Herman Melville's *Moby Dick,* reflects on this on the eve of his whaling trip. In the Bethel Chapel in New Bedford he looks at the black-bordered marble tablets that memorialize men "killed by a sperm whale on the coast of Japan . . . lost overboard near the isle of desolation near Patagonia . . . in a boat towed out of sight by a whale in the Pacific." At first he muses dolefully: "Yes, Ishmael, the same fate may be thine. . . . but somehow I grew merry again. . . . Methinks we have hugely mistaken this matter of Life and Death. Methinks what they call my shadow here on earth is my true substance. . . . In fact, take my body who will take it, I say, it is not me."

Apparently Ishmael was confident that if death overtook him, his God would be there to rescue his immortal soul. Though sailors are acknowledged to be a rough and tumble lot, underneath they were aware of the Hand that ruled the seas.

Dr. E. Stanley Jones, in his book *Growing Spiritually,* tells of a woman who felt intimations of this other life somewhat like Ishmael. She had just been in an automobile accident in which her husband had been killed and in which she, her two boys, and a sister-in-law were injured. Her letter read:

Brother Stanley, ever since a year ago at the silent Communion service, I've understood what death really is and have tried to tell others in a small degree just how beautiful an experience it will really be. It seemed to me at the Communion service I really got a glimpse of eternity and it was so beautiful my heart nearly broke with joy and rapture. . . . I wondered when my time came to "taste of death" if it would hit me as an evil thing, or if it would seem beautiful. . . . Now I can tell you with all truthfulness that my original opinion is strengthened.

As I turned away from the storm-littered beach, it was with thankfulness for these messages from others. When we are faced with the storms of life as well as the storms of nature, belief in a God that has dominion from sea to sea apparently helps.

Our Father whose kingdom stretches throughout the universe, we thank thee for thy power we see revealed in the natural world. Help us to take comfort in such power that extends not only throughout our physical world but on into the next spiritual existence; in Jesus' name. Amen.

Calamities of Nature

He stretched out his hand over the sea,
he shook the kingdoms.
                    —Isaiah 23:11a KJV

No one who lives near the sea can forget that calamities and disasters occasionally occur that are quite beyond the power of humans to stop or control. When a hurricane combined with high tides batters the coast, water sweeps over docks and low-lying houses; ships and buildings are tossed about like matchsticks. All humans can do is evacuate and wait for nature's powerful onslaught to subside.

Recorded history is full of these calamities, from the biblical flood to the recent Alaskan earthquake. One of the most dramatic that ever occurred happened in the last century in Indonesia. Exactly at 5:30 A.M. on August 27, 1883, residents for hundreds of miles around the volcanic island of Krakatoa were jolted awake by what sounded like the firing of heavy guns. While terrified people gathered in clusters "under a midnight black sky streaked with lightning from volcanic electrical storms generated from an eruption, a second explosion cracked foundations and scattered glass like confetti. Then came an indescribable roar and a blast that toppled houses and trees like Tinkertoys."

According to an article in the December, 1978, *Reader's Digest* by Emily and Pei Ola D'Aulaire, it was the loudest explosion ever heard by mankind. When the volcanic eruption occurred on the tiny island,

millions of tons of seawater gushed into the white hot interior of the planet, turned to superheated steam and shot up through the island, disintegrating most of it in a cataclysmic burst of power. Black clouds of ash, flaming desk-size blocks of pumice and obsidian from deep inside the earth shot upward at the speed of rockets 25 miles into the

117

atmosphere. Then most of the surface of the island slumped into the bowels of the earth and disappeared.

Australian residents 2,300 miles southeast heard the strange explosions while people 3,000 miles southwest on Rodriguez Island in the Indian Ocean were puzzled by the sound of what they thought were sounds of heavy guns. A great wave triggered by the eruption sped around the globe. At first 125 feet high, it leveled many coastal towns. Ships at sea were pummeled by glowing rocks and red-hot ash. Sailors were hard put to extinguish the fire. When it was over, more than 36,000 people had died, 300 Indonesian villages were gone, and 6,000 ships were smashed. For a year afterward, the dust in the atmosphere created strange and spectacular sunsets.

I wonder, as I read of these awesome events of both the long ago and today, what place these have in God's plan. There is no real answer to the toll of human lives and the terrible destruction of food and shelter that are needed for human survival. It is beyond my comprehension. One theologian tells us that God does not suspend or violate his established ways to save those who trust in him, because he "provides for human welfare through the constant, dependable functioning of the natural order."

What, then, is the lesson of these calamities? Probably it is to remind us of his awesome power lest we humans become too cocky, too sure of our own abilities. We are really frail and powerless, he reminds us, and our trust should be placed in the spiritual power of the world, not in the physical.

O God of Power, thou art Lord of all the earth including the awesome and catastrophic as well as the good and the beautiful. Help us to so place our trust in thee that even though kingdoms are shaken and calamities befall us we are upheld by thy love and care; in Jesus' name. Amen.

The Lowly Sponge

*So teach us to number our days, that
we may apply our hearts unto
wisdom.*
—Psalm 90:12 KJV

I have a friend who beachcombs each morning and evening in summertime. Her living room shelves are loaded with the multicolored results. Amid pastel shells, dried seaweed, and sea-smoothed pebbles are a few dainty sponges.

I often think about sponges. These animals cannot move around; do not have heart, lungs, or brain; possess no nervous system; and have no arms and legs to defend themselves. Yet the sponge has survived with little change for millions of years. Sponges inhabit all the world's oceans as well as freshwater streams and lakes. There are about five thousand species. They come in all colors and sizes. Some are as tiny as a kernel of corn. Others, like the barrel sponge, grow to a height of six feet.

These queer specimens of the underwater world have been a boon to mankind. Ancient Greeks and Romans used them as mops and paintbrushes as well as for pads in their armor. In succeeding centuries these helpful animals have mopped and polished constantly. We use them for those tasks today. I much prefer a natural sponge to a synthetic one for wiping my kitchen sink. Its ability to mop up many times its weight in water is an amazing attribute, one that I appreciate every time I sop up spilled liquid.

While doing so, my mind usually drifts to humans who are like sponges. Isaac Asimov is surely one. I marvel at how his mind files away anything he reads and returns it to his consciousness whenever he wishes it recalled. At last count his books numbered more than two hundred! I remember a visit he made to the Craigville Conference Center to participate in the Cape Cod Writers' Conference. Remaining a few days to vacation he attended a lecture on Petra, that red-rock city deep in the Arabian desert that had been "lost" to civilization for hundreds of years. Not many people know the story of the Nabataeans who peopled Petra at the time of Christ when it was an important caravan stop between Persia and Egypt. But Asimov was fully aware of the people and their history even though he had never been there. From the audience he embellished the comments of the lecturer, enriching the program for all who attended.

There have been others who have soaked up knowledge like sponges. Wolfgang Mozart, who was composing music and giving concerts prior to entering his teens, was one.

Although we cannot hope to be geniuses of the caliber of a person like Mozart or Asimov, we can certainly try to emulate the sponge. We can train ourselves to absorb what we read and hear, then use this information for the good of humankind. There are courses in memory training and speed reading. There are numerous how-to books on these subjects. The emphasis on meditation in recent years is excellent, for as folks reach deeper into their own subconscious, they release energies and abilities they never realized they possess.

Whenever I look at a lowly sponge, I determine to be more like it. I also realize that although the sponge does it automatically, I have to work at it. Perhaps this was in the mind of the psalmist when he urged us to "apply our hearts unto wisdom."

Father of all knowledge, we thank thee for the example of the lowly sponge. Increase in us the knowledge and wisdom that we need to release to the world many times over the information and help we now possess; in Jesus' name. Amen.

A Vessel of Papyrus

Ah, land of whirring wings . . .
which sends ambassadors . . . in
vessels of papyrus upon the waters.
—Isaiah 18:1-2

Until 1970, most of us thought a vessel of reeds was something that existed only in long-ago scripture. Then Thor Heyerdahl built a ship of papyrus reeds held together with only rope and crossed the Atlantic Ocean. Those who observed the construction of *RA II*, which took place in a garden in Safi, Morocco, probably shook their heads at the explorer's plan. They recalled that *RA I* couldn't complete its voyage the previous year because the stern broke. But Heyerdahl was confident that the construction of the first reed vessel was at fault, not the concept. If fishermen in Lake Chad in Africa can sail reed boats today and if similarly designed papyrus boats are also sailed by Indians of Peru and Bolivia in South America, then prehistoric voyagers could have sailed across the Atlantic, he reasoned. How else do we account for the similarities of ancient civilizations of both continents—for sun worshipers, pyramids, giant statues, hieroglyphics, mummification, and cranial surgery that existed in both places.

Setting out on May 10, 1970, the tiny "golden ark" reached Barbados in the West Indies fifty-seven days later, proving such an ancient voyage could indeed have taken place. Flying the flag of the United Nations, the eight-man crew of many nations, colors, and creeds proved also that these differences do not prevent men's cooperating. "Man is man, wherever you find him; I feel he cannot be divided or united according to height, color, or pencil lines on a map," said Heyerdahl. "We attributed our success to cooperation among men of many nations who learned that no space is too narrow, no stress too great, if men will join hands for common survival."

121

Many of us echo these findings recorded by this distinguished explorer who in 1947 sailed the *Kon Tiki* from South America to Polynesia to prove that ancient Peruvians could have contributed to South Sea culture. We rejoice that the much decorated, award-winning Heyerdahl has amply used his knowledge and skills for the advancement of mankind.

But what can people like us do when contrasted with these great achievers? Not much, it seems; yet that is not what Jesus said. In the parable of the talents Jesus assured us that those who have one talent as well as those who have five are equally important. We know of a five-talent man. Albert Schweitzer was outstanding in music, theology, medicine, philosophy, and literature. Like Heyerdahl he has contributed immeasurably to our civilization. But Jesus said one-talent people are important too, as long as they don't bury their gifts but put them to use. If we use our one talent to the best of our ability, then we are doing all that God expects of us. We are fulfilling our destiny.

So we must pick up our pen, our scalpel, our sermon, our lesson plan, or whatever vehicle is ours to use. Even though we do not sail vessels of papyrus or become five-talent people, we are doing an important and needed service in the world.

Our Father God, enable us to understand what our talents and mission are in life. Then help us to develop them, whether they be one or five, in the service of our neighbors; in Jesus' name. Amen.

Underwater Habitat

He maketh the sea like a pot of
ointment.
—Job 41:31 KJV

Little did the psalmist know, when he sang praises to God of the wondrous works in the deep, how amazing the activities would be under the sea in the twentieth century. In this era the age-old terror and fright of the ocean are being turned into appreciation, sometimes as soothing as Job's "pot of ointment." I am thinking of the underwater habitat developed by oceanographer Jacques-Yves Cousteau. In 1963, French oceanauts lived for a month in a submerged colony thirty-six feet underneath the surface of the Red Sea. In Starfish House, five men were sheltered adequately for these thirty days. While living there, they dived to even greater depths and performed many experiments to determine if ocean-bottom laboratories are possible.

I find it hard to believe this, as I look across the expansive ocean; yet I know that more recent underwater habitats have been even more elaborate. In 1970 United States government agencies cooperated in Tektite II, which was located in Great Lameshur Bay in the Virgin Islands. In this twin-towered structure placed fifty feet below the sea's surface, five teams of scientists, including one all-woman group, were successively housed. All the comforts of home were provided—television, wall-to-wall carpeting, air conditioning, an electric stove, and a freshwater shower. In addition, the panoramic windows gave a magnificent view of the gargantuan swimming pool and fantastic aquarium. The National Aeronautic and Space Administration is using the resulting observations of isolated living in planning future space missions. Oceanographers are looking forward to marine-science classes being conducted under water. "Submarine farming, effective monitoring of the ocean, undersea mining and industrial work all seem closer at hand now that habitats have proven possible, practical devices," wrote Dr. Sylvia Earle in the August, 1971, issue of *The National Geographic.*

Now that humans are delving deeply into the last great frontier, the sea, and finding new life patterns, I wonder if the descent into the uncharted depths of the spiritual world will keep pace. Surely there is much in the unseen world yet to be discovered that will benefit humans. We have hints of this through the writings of people with the gift of healing. There is Emily Gardner Neal, for example, newspaper reporter who went to cover a healing service and witnessed a miracle that changed her life. Others who are documented healers are Olga Worrell and Agnes Sanford.

Once when Mrs. Sanford was visiting a scientist's wife for the purpose of healing, the woman commented on the feeling of inner heat that followed the healing prayer. "I can believe that," said the scientist as quoted in Mrs. Sanford's book *The Healing Light,*

because my studies in the vibrations of sight and sound have shown me that such a thing must be. In the course of our experiments we have come to the conclusion that a vibration of very, very high intensity and on an extremely fine wave-length with tremendous power, caused by spiritual forces operating through the mind of man, is the next thing science expects to discover.

Surely if habitats in the natural world can exist where even a few decades ago such "amazing happenings" could not even be imagined, then similar explorations shall produce wonders in the spiritual world.

Father of all worlds—inward, outward, natural, and spiritual—help us to understand all your worlds better. Give us the

imagination and the courage to delve deeper into these worlds,
providing more effective habitats physically and spiritually; in
Jesus' name. Amen.

Luminescence

Come, let us walk
in the light of the Lord.
—Isaiah 2:5*b*

How mysterious the sea is at night! As we walk the beach on a summer evening, wavelets lap the shore quietly, and soft breezes touch our cheeks. Over the water, buoy lights are flashing at intervals, and the stars above seem close enough to touch. The moon lays a silver path. These are comforting lights, ones that are familiar and explainable.

Then come other lights not so easily explained. It is almost as if there were a trail of phosphorescent light in the water. Myriads of tiny algae cause this, we are told. The effect is much stronger in tropical waters, I understand, where the moon, stars, and luminescent organisms combine to give a surprising amount of light.

I recall reading an account by Robert Schroeder of night diving off Lower Matecumbe Key, seventy miles south of Miami, Florida. He noted:

These luminescent organisms are the most beautiful phenomena on the reefs. On moonlit nights there is enough light to dive without head lamps and the luminescence of many creatures becomes apparent. Any disturbance results in a shower of sparks from luminous dinoflagellates, and swimming worms and jellies glow with periodic brilliance. Lights race up and down the arms of plankton-fishing brittle stars, and the underside of an overturned rock sparkles like the embers of a dying fire.

Sometimes luminous microscopic organisms concentrate in such numbers that fish and divers are outlined in a cool green light.

As I watch this phosphorescence on our sea, I reflect on the number of times Jesus used light to symbolize his message of good news and to explain the kingdom of God. "Ye are the light of the world," he said. I think also of the many times the word *light* is used to describe Jesus. "In him was the life, and the life was the light of men. The Light shines in the darkness, and the darkness has not overcome it." John the Baptist heralded Jesus' coming by saying, "The true light that enlightens every man was coming into the world."

As I turned homeward I thought of the lighthouses that dot our coast. These are beacons that warn of treacherous shoals and give the ship good news of its whereabouts. Perhaps if Jesus had lived by the sea, he might have said, "The kingdom of God is like a lighthouse set high on a bluff for all to see."

One message of this luminous night is clear. Lights are important. We must keep our lights polished and shining so that we will be lights as Jesus commanded. Our lights must be beacons of hope in an uneasy and threatening world. We must walk so closely in the light of our Lord that his light will be seen in us.

Father of all lights, we thank thee for the luminescence of the sea that reminds us how important lights are. Keep us ever close to thee so that we will carry your light of hope to all we meet, in Jesus' name. Amen.

God's Bonus Days

Sing to the Lord a new song,
his praise from the end of the earth!
—Isaiah 42:10a

My heart is sad today. The golden summer is ended. The trees are dressed in crimson. The air is sharp as if warning of the impending winter. I can no longer revel in warm breezes at the beach. The winds are more strident now as they tug at my hair and jacket.

Still, how much more fortunate am I than those who must leave these shores for an inland home when vacation days are over. For them the sea will be only a distant memory, while I can still see the ocean through the glass wall of my living room. In the distance I will be able to watch the inexorable march of the waves toward the beach. At night I will be able to note the blinking buoys that year round warn of dangerous shoals.

I am determined to remember the closeness to the water I have felt in summer, just as those far away will turn to seaside memories with nostalgia. These reminders will help us to live through the waiting until it is beach-time again.

My nostalgic day in winter might be a brisk beach walk while I am wrapped in a cocoon of wool. Others farther away might recall seaside experiences through vacation photographs or a good book about the sea. There are plenty of books from which to choose. The current volume of *Books in Print* lists at least one thousand sea-related volumes, and it is estimated that there are three thousand still available in America. This doesn't, of course, count those long-out-of-print books nestled on library or private shelves.

An author writing in *Guideposts* magazine calls these nostalgic times of memory "God's bonus days." LaVerne

127

Saxton recalled that in her family life's unexpected dividends—like a summer rainbow, a glorious sunset, a warm spring thaw—were occasions for shedding mundane tasks for a special event. She remembers one sensationally beautiful day in her childhood when the incredibly blue vault of the sky seemed limitless. Her dad picked up fishing poles and called, "Let's play hookey, hon. It's one of God's bonus days."

I like this idea. I think I shall take a bonus day every so often and revive my seaside memories.

Suddenly I am illumined with an idea. This longing for the sea has a parallel in the inner longing we have for God's way. Augustine said it best when he wrote, "Our hearts are restless until they rest in thee." Though we may attend church regularly, read the Bible often, and turn to God daily in prayer, sometimes our busyness makes these actions mechanical. Our mind may be elsewhere as we proceed along our habitual way. Perhaps we should have bonus days for things of the Spirit too. It might be a weekend retreat, a quiet day of reflection spent by ourselves, or perhaps the study of an unusually provocative book.

The sea and our inner life are unfathomable, unlimited, full of secrets. They tug at our heart in ways we cannot always understand or express. All we know is that we must turn toward them and learn as much as we can about them while we walk life's pilgrimage. God's bonus days might be a very special aid in this endeavour. The very thought of them makes me rejoice. I am sad no longer. I will "sing unto the Lord a new song."

Almighty God, who is the Lord of the outward as well as the inward sea, help us to understand more and more of their mysteries. Guide us to use this understanding in ways that will benefit mankind and help us to praise you always; in Jesus' name. Amen.

Printed in the United States
64626LVS00001B/67-84